IS COFFEE BREAK THE
BEST PART OF YOUR DAY?

DICK LEATHERMAN

Published by HRD Press, Inc.
    22 Amherst Road
    Amherst, Massachusetts 01002
    1-800-822-2801

First Printing September, 1990

ISBN 0-87425-040-0

Production Services by Susan Kotzin

This book is dedicated to Randy Johnson,
a United Parcel Service truck driver.

He is one of the most dedicated individuals I have ever known.
He has a fantastic attitude about his job,
and he provides us with exemplary service.

When I think of how this country has become great,
I think of people like Randy.

Grateful acknowledgment is made to the following individuals who read the rough draft of this book and then offered valuable ideas to make the final version even better:

- Del Boerner — Personnel Services Manager, County of San Diego, California
- Joanne DeMark — Director of National Education, H.B.O. & Company, Atlanta, Georgia
- Ken Grieve — Corporation Human Resource Development Manager, Oscar Mayer Foods, Madison, Wisconsin
- Leonard Hill — Manager of Executive Development, AMP, Inc., Harrisburg, Pennsylvania
- Linda Herrig — Manager of OD & Training, Ore-Ida, Inc., Boise, Idaho
- Jim Houlditch — Vice President, Texas Instruments, Dallas, Texas
- Dennis and Dianne LaMountain — Consultants, Richmond, Virginia
- Denise Leblond — Training & Development Officer, Civil Service Coop., Ottawa, Canada
- Robert Newman — Training & Development Officer, Toronto Transit, Toronto, Canada
- Roger Pelkey — Manager of Training & Development, Elco Ind., Inc., Rockford, Illinois
- Mohan Rao — Senior Vice President, Semi-Conductor Group, Texas Instruments, Dallas, Texas
- Steve Rouch — Manager of Human Resource Development, Commonwealth Aluminum, Lewisport, Kentucky
- Carol L. Smith — Author, Richmond, Virginia

- Charlie Sweet — Director of Training & Development, Utica National Insurance, New Hartford, New York
- Arlan Tietal — Training Manager, 3-M Company, St. Paul, Minnesota
- Deirdre Weisbach — Consultant, Chatham, New Jersey
- Craig Woodacre — Manager of Training, Bristol-Myers, Syracuse, New York

And special thanks to:

- David McKnight for his herculean efforts in proofing my grammar, syntax, and punctuation.
- Bill Griffin, Professor of English, Virginia Commonwealth University, for the final editing of this manuscript.
- Shirley Foutz, Literacy Specialist, Richmond Newspapers, and Betsy Weaver, Chesterfield County Schools, for their work in making this book more readable.

My thanks also to Nancy Leatherman, M.D., wife and friend, for the title of this book. From her I have learned much about life—which is what this book is all about.

CONTENTS

CONTENTS

iii

INTRODUCTION

If you're tired of feeling that work is drudgery, then this book is for you. It's a distilled, boiled-down explanation of how you can become the best you can be—and have fun doing it! But there is a catch. You'll no longer be able to blame your feelings about your job or your performance on your organization, boss, or co-workers. Why not? Because YOU are responsible for the joy you find in your work! Not your boss, co-worker, or spouse. You!

Something interesting begins to happen when you really take responsibility for yourself. You work better. You become more effective. And when you become as productive as you can be, you will find that work becomes pleasure. It's a wonderful cycle. The better you perform, the more you will enjoy what you do. And the more you enjoy your work, the better you become at it. And what's more—society rewards people who become more effective at what they do.

Sure, life could always be easier. Bosses could be better bosses. The organization probably could make some changes that would make your job less difficult. But as long as you expect others to change, you won't do much about yourself. And there ARE things you can do almost immediately to become an outstanding employee—no matter what kind of crazy organization you work for. And when you become an outstanding employee, you don't have to work for crazy organizations. You can work anywhere you want to—with joy!

There are two things that will make your job more fun. One is to know as much as you can about the job. The second is to be effective. By "effective" I mean an employee who uses his or her head, has good work habits, and gets along with others. Job knowledge and effectiveness—it takes both to be successful. And successful people are the ones who arrange their jobs to be fun.

There are exceptions, of course. If you are the only person in your organization who can operate the old computer that was installed twenty years ago, then you don't have to be particularly effective in dealing with others—until the day that they replace that old computer. But *outstanding* employees need not only to learn their job, they also need to learn how to be effective.

Sometimes we're fortunate in being able to learn how to be effective by having a competent boss, or effective parents. But many of us aren't so lucky. We may even have had incompetent bosses, or less than effective parents. So we never had the opportunity to learn what it means to take responsibility for ourselves, to become the best that we can be. That's what this book is all about.

I remember my first job—as a plumber's helper. How I hated that job! But I became pretty good at unclogging stopped-up commodes, digging ditches, and threading pipe. In other words, I got so I could do the job. But I was still a lousy employee! I goofed off, took long coffee breaks (coffee breaks were definitely the best part of my job), even longer lunch breaks, and always looked for ways of getting out of work. The only reason I kept the job that summer was that the owner was my uncle.

The following summer, my mother persuaded him to take me back. This time, I was assigned to work with Ike. Ike was the hardest-working person I'd ever seen—and one of the happiest. Forced by necessity to keep up with him, I became more productive. And as I became more productive, I began to feel great satisfaction in being competent. And the more competent I became, the more I enjoyed my job. So from Ike, I learned what it really meant to work. Not in terms of job knowledge; I already knew how to do the job. Ike taught me work habits. He became my model of what it meant to work. And what I learned that summer many years ago has become a deep part of me ever since.

So this book is for those of you who never had a chance to work for an "Ike."

Chapter 1
THE ATTITUDE OPPORTUNITY

You can't smell or taste an attitude. Attitudes are intangible. But most people know instinctively what good—and bad—attitudes "look" like. You recognize attitudes by what people say or do. In general, if they speak well about their organization and their jobs, they are showing a good attitude. If their work shows little effort because they don't care about their job, they probably have a bad attitude.

What you see in others are symptoms. Often, it is difficult to really know what is going on inside them. You see their behaviors, draw conclusions about their attitudes, and even guess at how they are feeling. But all too often you don't know *why* they feel the way they feel.

However, you can look inside of yourself. It isn't always easy; but you can frequently figure out why you feel the way you feel. If you think you might have an "attitude opportunity"—that is, there's room for improvement—here is a six-step method you can use to understand what is going on—and fix it. And at the end of this chapter, there are work sheets you can use to help you improve your attitude.

First, here is an overview of the six steps. Ask yourself the questions:

1. What am I doing?

2. How did I feel?

3. Why did I feel that way?

4. What am I going to do?

5. How do I monitor my progress?

6. How do I reward myself for changing?

Now, let's look at each of these steps in more detail.

Step 1: WHAT AM I DOING?

What are you doing that might make someone say, "Boy, do you have attitude opportunity!"? Write down your answer. Be as specific as possible. It might help to ask yourself: "What are the things I do or say that show an attitude which needs improving?" You may need to list several things to describe your attitude opportunity.

If you are not sure what to write, ask some people you know at work how they see your attitude toward your job. But this can be both easy and difficult. It's easy, because all you have to do is ask the right person—your boss, or a trusted friend who knows you and your job performance. But it can also be hard to ask another person for constructive criticism. It's hard because it may force you to face something you might not want to face. And it's hard because most people simply don't like getting negative feedback.

Part of the answer lies in how you ask for feedback. If you ask, "Do I seem to have a bad attitude about my job?" the focus is on the negative side of your behavior. A better question is, "Do you see any ways I could improve my attitude on the job?" This is a positive way of asking the same question—and it will produce positive suggestions rather than a review of your negative behavior.

When you get an answer to your question, do your best not to become defensive. You simply want the truth—not a chance to explain yourself to others. Listen. Avoid interrupting. And ask for examples to help the person giving the feedback be more specific. Then, if possible, ask a second key person the same question to see if he or she has similar suggestions.

Step 2: HOW DID I FEEL?

When you did—or said—the things you described in Step 1 above, how did you really feel? Angry? Hurt? Depressed? Write these feelings down. Sometimes Step 2 is harder than you might think. Things happen, and if your feelings about them are not expressed or get buried, it may be hard to figure out later what you are feeling. Sometimes you will need help with this one—a counselor, minister, or simply a friend who's a good listener.

Step 3: WHY DID I FEEL THAT WAY?

Now, write your answer to this question. You may feel the way you feel for several reasons. 1) You may feel strongly about something because of similar things that happened in the past. 2) You may feel a certain way because of things that are happening outside of the job. 3) Or your attitude may in fact be a reaction to the way your organization is operating. Let's look at each of these in turn.

Past experiences. Your past experiences in life affect the way you see things today. In fact, such experiences can have a great impact on your present feelings. But the past may not be in your conscious thoughts even though you are affected by it. So when you first attempt to answer the question, "Why do I feel the way I do?" you will most often think of recent events. And these events are usually what somebody or something did to you.

But if you give yourself time to think more deeply, you may be able to remember a similar situation that occurred in your past—even in your childhood. This is not to say that a recent event isn't an important cause of your feelings. But the *intensity* of your reactions can sometimes only be fully explained by a similar negative experience— or experiences—at a previous time in your life.

Here is a personal example:

Many years ago, I took a field sales job at a *Fortune* 500 company. After several years went by, I developed what anybody would have said was a "bad attitude." I was late turning in my monthly expense forms. And there were days when I didn't even make my sales calls. I didn't stay home, because I would have been embarrassed to admit to anyone that I had a problem with my job. So I'd either force myself to make sales calls on old accounts where I felt accepted, or just go somewhere and get a cup of coffee.

When I ask the "Why?" question—Step 3 above—it is obvious why I didn't like the work I was doing. I didn't enjoy making sales calls because:

1) I felt as if I was "imposing" myself on my clients; and

2) I couldn't stand the frequent rejection—which I took personally.

I was sensitive to feelings of rejection because as a chubby teenager, my high school years were miserable. Because I was late in developing physically, I walked my high school halls in fear of being pounded by the bigger guys. When I was in my third year, I began to see that there were other guys who didn't get pounded even though they weren't jocks. They were the nice guys—the popular guys. So I made a career out of being nice. And it worked. I no longer got pounded in the hallways.

As a young salesperson, I still felt a little like the fat kid. I wanted to be liked, and the way to be liked was to be nice to people. But sometimes my customers weren't nice. They didn't buy my products, for whatever reason—and I took it personally!

Why didn't I quit? There were two reasons, one obvious and one hidden. First, there was a small part of my job that I really enjoyed—training new sales people. And because I enjoyed that part of my job, I spent quality time in preparing and conducting on-the-job training with them. But the real reason I didn't quit my job concerned my father, who was a salesman.

A sales career was something I admired about my father—and later thought he admired in me. That made it hard for me to accept the fact that I really wasn't cut out for sales.

So past experience had led to a career choice that had placed me in a job I didn't like—and at that time I didn't understand the real cause of my attitude problem.

Fortunately, the story had a happy ending. I wasn't fired. I was promoted—to a full-time training job that I really enjoyed, and performed well!

Outside causes. Many things that cause an "attitude problem" have nothing to do with the job itself. For example, if you are experiencing a marital separation or divorce, or even if you've just had a bad fight with your spouse, it's hard to be excited about your job. If your on-the-job attitude is a result of a serious problem off the job, it is best to get help. Talk to a counselor, or to your minister, rabbi, or priest. Or check to see if your organization has an employee assistance program. There is nothing shameful about seeking help when you are faced with what seems to be an overwhelming problem.

Organizational causes. In some cases, one's organization can cause problems. For example, I once worked for an individual who encouraged cheating on company expense vouchers. I was told to "hide" a legitimate business expense by claiming it was something other than what it really was. Even though the company was not actually being cheated, I didn't feel good about it. But my boss insisted I do it anyway. As a result, even though he was in many ways a competent manager, my negative attitude toward him made it difficult for me to accept his advice and counsel in other areas.

In another case, I know an employee whose work values are different from those of his organization. He feels that working 45 hours a week is more than enough. But his organization has no qualms about asking him to work 50, 60 and even 70 hours per week. This individual is *NOT* going to change his organization's values. And he cannot accept working 60 or more hours per week. As long as he continues to stay with this organization, he will have difficulty with his attitude.

After analyzing why you feel the way you do, the next step is to take action to resolve the situation by turning it into an opportunity.

Step 4: WHAT AM I GOING TO DO?

In some cases, taking action will simply mean deciding to change your outward behavior—and you may have to make an effort. If you seldom get to work on time in the morning, then start coming to work on time! If you are a constant complainer, then stop complaining. This may sound too simple. But for the most part, you *DO* have control over what you do or say. And you *CAN* take responsibility for your outward symptoms—and create an opportunity for positive change!

Sometimes simply changing your outward behavior can produce such good results that you may not need to dig deeper to find other causes of an attitude problem. But more often, if you are looking for a permanent solution to a problem, you will need to better understand what you're feeling, why you are feeling it, and then take action to fix the underlying causes of the problem. In my case, the trouble was solved when I was promoted to a job I immediately liked. But suppose I hadn't been promoted? Knowing what I know now, the best way for me to have handled my situation would have been to analyze more deeply the "What?" and "Why?" of my negative feelings—and then to share with my father what I had discovered about myself. I know now that he would have been flattered by my reason for choosing a sales career. He would have advised me to look for a job I enjoyed doing. And he would have felt pleased that I chose to confide in him.

Step 5:   HOW DO I MONITOR MY PROGRESS?

Your goal here will be to build habits that will help you maintain constant improvement. Since by now you have a good understanding of the behaviors that need improvement, it will be easy to measure your progress toward correcting them. For example, if you are consistently late for work, and decide to be on time in the future, keep an attendance log on your desk calendar for several months, noting the time you arrive at work each day. You may even want to strengthen your commitment by sharing your plans with your boss or co-worker.

Step 6:   HOW DO I REWARD MYSELF FOR CHANGING?

Reward yourself when you change your behavior for the better. If you tell your supervisor you plan to make a change, and do so—then tell him or her when you have successfully reached your goal. Or pick a trusted friend, tell him or her about your plans, and ask for positive feedback when you exhibit a changed attitude.

A good attitude about your job is essential for success and satisfaction—and to happiness at home! If you suspect that you have an opportunity to improve your attitude, do something about it. If you don't, the person who is hurt the most is you. The simple steps above will literally work miracles in changing bad attitudes to good ones, and frustration to job happiness.

The Attitude Opportunity Check Sheet

1. **WHAT AM I DOING?**

    A. What am I doing (or not doing), and saying (or not saying) that may be perceived as an "attitude opportunity"? I'll need to be specific.

        _____

        _____

        _____

    B. What have others said about my attitude?

        _____

        _____

    C. Whom could I ask to give me honest feedback?

        _____

    D. What question(s) could I ask this person? (For example, "What specific things should I do or say that will demonstrate an improved attitude?" Remember to word the question so as to receive positive suggestions, not negative criticism. Ask for examples.)

        _____

        _____

        _____

    E. Write a summary of what this individual said.

        _____

        _____

        _____

        _____

2. HOW DID I FEEL?

When I originally did or said what I wrote in Step 1A, how did
I really feel?

_____

_____

3. WHY DID I FEEL THAT WAY?

_____

_____

_____

What experience or experiences have I had in the past that may
have influenced the way I felt?

_____

_____

_____

4. WHAT AM I GOING TO DO?

What action(s) will I take to eliminate the symptom (behaviors)
of my past attitude?

_____

_____

_____

If I found an underlying cause of my attitude, was it an outside
cause or an organizational cause? _____

Given I know the cause, what can I do to resolve the situation?

_____

_____

_____

5. **HOW DO I MONITOR MY PROGRESS?**

   How do I plan to monitor my progress as I change my attitude?

   _____
   _____
   _____

6. **HOW DO I REWARD MYSELF FOR CHANGING?**

   How do I plan to reward myself when I successfully change?

   _____
   _____
   _____

CHAPTER 2
HOW TO BENEFIT FROM CRITICISM

"**Ox·y·mo·ron:** a figure of speech in which opposite or contradictory ideas or terms are combined (Ex: thunderous silence, sweet sorrow)." *Webster's Dictionary.*

Like the example above, "constructive criticism" is a figure of speech that tends to appear contradictory. "Criticism" often is, or appears to be, destructive—not constructive. You get "destructive criticism" from family, friends, peers and bosses. It happens in meetings, in the hallway, over the phone, and in your home. There's no escaping it! Therefore, you need to cope with criticism in ways that will make it constructive.

In this chapter, the person who gives the criticism will be discussed, as well as your role as the receiver of criticism. You will also see a step-by-step method for handling criticism. And finally, there is a work sheet at the end of the chapter that you can use to evaluate the times when you felt criticized.

The sender. Let's look first at the sender, or giver, of criticism. You know that it makes a great difference *who* is criticizing you. But even more important than who is criticizing you is their *motive* for doing so. If you sense that they are not motivated by a sincere desire to help, you probably won't listen to what they have to say. If they are angry, for instance, you may feel angry in response. Or if they normally criticize everything and everybody, you may question the validity of what they say. And if you sense that their motive is to prove you're "wrong," you won't be very receptive.

When you are criticized can also make a difference. You have probably had days when you felt overloaded and stressed beyond your ability to cope. Criticism given at this time may seem almost more than you can bear.

Finally, *where* the criticism takes place can also have an impact on how you receive it. For example, criticism given in front of others is usually much harder to accept than if it is expressed in private.

The receiver. How well you handle criticism can depend on the perceived motive of the sender, when the criticism is given, and where it occurs. But come it will—and then what? How do you make the best of criticism?

First, remember that you do have the right to say "No" to criticism. For example, if the time or place is truly inappropriate, then you can ask the sender to hold his or her comments for a more suitable time or place. You might say, "Thank you for pointing that out. Since I feel uncomfortable with others present, would it be possible to finish this discussion later?" If it is your boss who is criticizing you in front of others, it may sound a bit bold to ask your boss to continue his or her criticism at another time or place. But in most cases, this suggestion will be accepted.

Second, the problem of dealing with criticism is that there is usually a bit (or even more than a bit!) of truth in what the sender is saying. And if you care about what is being said, it is that bit of truth that hurts. For example: A friend of mine was raised at a time when the "man" was the "head of the household." The man's responsibility was to provide for his family. So even though his wife earned a good living, he was sensitive to his "traditional" role of supporting the family—through hard work. Therefore, if he spent a workday doing non-work-related activities, he felt a little uneasy. After all, by his values he should be working to support his family.

Recently when his wife asked him to take a day off to do something with her, his reaction was "Oh no, that's a *work*day!" She, feeling rejected and a little angry, responded by saying, "You took a day off last week to do what you wanted to do. So why can't you take a day off to do what I want to do?" Because what she said was partly true, he got upset. It took him awhile to calm down and accept what she said, and agree to take the day off.

Now let's look at some ways you can manage criticism at the workplace.

First, accept that what you do in the face of criticism is up to you. You are seldom going to change the way others give you criticism. (Not that it can't be done; but it isn't likely.) Therefore, it's often easier to manage your own reactions to the criticism than it is to manage the way the sender is giving it.

Second, realize also that the criticism is true as perceived by the other person. It is rare that people criticize without believing in the correctness of their criticism.

Third, it is also true that people will sometimes be irritated, or even angry, when giving criticism. A person may well be upset at being put in a position of having to criticize you. In addition, he or she may well have been criticized by his or her boss. "After all," the other person thinks, "who needs this hassle! I've got enough to do without having to put up with a problem that would never have been a problem if you hadn't messed up."

But to become angry because someone else is angry won't help. Rather, you need to handle the criticism in a way that will help you understand what you actually did, what you shouldn't have done (or didn't do that you should have), and what you need to do to correct the situation.

Finally, if you really want to take the responsibility for your own growth, seek out criticism (or feedback) from others. In other words, be proactive, not always reactive. By appropriately asking others, you will be able to control who gives you feedback, where and when it occurs, and the subject of the feedback.

Handling criticism. Now let's look at some strategies for handling criticism constructively when emotions are strong.

1. **Listen! Listen intently.** And as you listen, look at the person who is criticizing you. Don't think of what you are going to say in response to what you are hearing. Simply look, listen— and don't interrupt.

   Listening is the most powerful strategy you have for handling criticism. It's powerful for three reasons.

   - First, the more the other person talks, the more information you will have.
   - Second, the more he or she talks, the lower will be his or her level of emotion. (Try this strategy the next time someone is irritated or angry with you. Notice how hard it is for that individual to stay angry—if you simply listen without interrupting.)
   - And third, if you realize that what you should do at this point is listen, you won't waste energy getting mad, or thinking about how you can best defend yourself.

2. **Paraphrase what you believe you heard**. If you can repeat, in your own words, what you think you heard, you will communicate clearly that you really did listen to what was said— and that you understood it. If you did *not* understand the

criticism, the other person will let you know by giving you more information, or simply by repeating the original criticism. This will also give you time to mentally relax, listen carefully, and further reduce your level of emotion.

For example, suppose my boss, Bill, walks through the office, stops at my desk and says, "Dick, you have the messiest desk in the department. It always looks like a pigpen. Look at the lousy example you set for your subordinates! How can you expect your people to keep their areas clean when your desk looks so disorganized?"

Let's look at the facts. First, my desk is messy. In fact, it's usually messy (though not always—I remember cleaning it off six months ago). None of my subordinates' desks are messy. They are generally well-organized, and their desks are normally neat and clean. But I also am the best manager my boss has, and my messy desk has not interfered with my production or leadership.

So my instinctive response to my boss's criticism is to say, "Now wait just a minute! My desk isn't *always* messy. The last time I cleaned it off you didn't say a word. You didn't even notice. And not only that, all four of my people keep their desks cleaner than yours! So how can it be that my people are modeling their desk habits after me—or you?"

The point here is that you can almost always find some element of untruth in a criticism, and attack that part of what was said. But don't do it! Arguing your case may work well in a courtroom, but it won't help in handling constructive criticism. It only makes the other person feel that you are not taking seriously what he or she said—which will usually raise his or her emotional level.

It would be far better for me to listen intently, without interrupting. Then I can paraphrase what I heard by saying, "Bill, I can see you are really upset over the condition of my desk, because you feel that a good manager should be a good model for his subordinates. Is that correct?"

Notice that I acknowledged his feelings ("I can see you are really upset"), stated in my own words what he was upset about ("the condition of my desk"), rephrased why he felt upset ("a good manager should be a good model for his subordinates"), and closed by asking if what I heard was correct ("Is that correct?"). My response had four components:

1. Acknowledgment of observed feelings.
2. A restatement of the criticism.
3. The reason(s) why he or she was upset.
4. A question to confirm my understanding.

Notice also that I did not become defensive. And I did not even attack that part of his statement that was incorrect (i.e., I did not mention the fact that my subordinates' desks, all neat and clean, had not been affected by my "lousy example").

3. **If necessary, ask questions to gain more information.** In the illustration above, for example, I could have asked for more specific information about the messy desk, and then asked more questions about what he expected the desk to look like. Questions like, "What in particular about my desk bothers you the most?" or, "How, specifically, do you want my desk to look?" In the example above, of course, I knew what he meant by "a messy desk"; and I also knew what he wanted it to look like! So I didn't need to ask information questions. Instead, I moved directly to Step 4.

4. **Ask "action" questions.** Action questions probe for ideas as to what should be done to correct the problem. In the example above, I might ask questions like, "What ideas do you have about how I can keep my desk cleaner?" Or, "What suggestions do you have as to how I could organize my desk so that it doesn't get messy?" Of course, I may already have seen how to correct the problem. But involving the other person in

developing a solution communicates clearly my desire to change my behavior.

5. **Commit to doing something.** Make a decision to do at least one important thing to remedy the situation. In the above example, I could agree to begin by removing the stack of papers that always sits in the middle of my desk. There are probably a number of things I can do to improve my desk. And whatever I do will take time. But if I commit to doing one key thing to improve the situation, there is a much better chance that I will be inspired to take the next step, and the next, until the goal is achieved.

6. **Devise ways to ensure that the change is permanent.** People are creatures of habit: they tend to revert to old ways of doing things unless there are built-in strategies to keep this from happening. For example, there are a number of things I could do to ensure my success in my clean desk project. I could bet my subordinates $10 that I could keep my desk clean for a month (they would love to take my money). Or, I could take a "before and after" picture of my desk, and post it on the bulletin board. Do whatever works; and what works depends on you!

Receiving criticism is not easy. But if you remember that there is probably some truth in the criticism you receive, you can resolve to understand that truth and make needed changes.

CHECK SHEET
HOW TO BENEFIT FROM CRITICISM

Think of the last time someone criticized you. Analyze below how
you handled the criticism.

1. How well did I listen without interrupting? _____
    _____
    _____
    _____

2. Did I paraphrase what I thought I heard? _____
    If "yes," did I: 1) acknowledge the other person's feelings;
    2) restate the criticism that I heard; 3) describe the reasons
    why he or she was upset; and, 4) ask a question to confirm the
    accuracy of my response? _____

    Did I refrain from becoming defensive? _____
    From attacking perceived weaknesses in the criticism?_____

3. Did I ask questions to gain more information? _____
    What questions did I ask? _____
    _____
    _____

4. Did I ask questions to involve the giver of the criticism to develop
    a solution that is suitable for both of us? _____
    _____

    What questions did I ask? _____
    _____
    _____

    If not, what questions could I have asked? _____
    _____
    _____

5. Did I commit to doing something? _____
   Did I commit to doing too much? _____
   What should I have committed to do? _____
   _____
   _____

6. If I committed to doing something, has the change become
   permanent? _____
   If not, what can I do to ensure that the change is permanent?
   _____
   _____
   _____

CHAPTER 3
COMMUNICATIONS—
ARE YOU LISTENING?

Speaking and listening: two major components of communications—and of life! And yet how few of us have had formal training in these two all-important areas. We've studied history, math, English, spelling, geography. But who ever had a "speaking" book? And how many hours did we spend doing "listening" homework? So how can we learn to communicate? Mostly from life's experiences. Good experiences. Bad experiences.

Experience has taught us what to do and what not to do. Unfortunately, some of the things we have learned about communication may not be the most effective ways of doing it. Since this is such a critical skill, it is important that we take a look at how we presently communicate—and be willing to modify our behavior if needed.

Although numerous books are available on the subject of communications in business, the majority were written for speakers, counselors, supervisors, and managers. And most of those few aimed at employees are overly basic. The following helpful ideas are directed specifically to you, and they take a different approach!

You communicate with two main groups on the job—your bosses and your co-workers. Conversations with bosses are usually "situational"—that is, they reflect the situation you are in. For example, you talk with your boss when being appraised, receiving assignments, being counseled for a performance problem, or reviewing career goals. These types of situations are covered in detail in other sections of this book. The purpose of this chapter is to examine how you communicate with your co-workers.

There are a number of ways to look at oral communication. But for our purpose, we will use a model to help explain what communication is. By using a model, we can establish a language to talk about—and understand—the way people communicate. A model can also help those of us who, like me, learn better graphically.

Let's first look at the three primary elements in the model, the "Sender," "Message," and "Receiver."

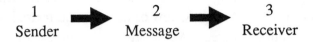

In its simplest form, the model shows that 1) someone 2) says something 3) to somebody. I wish it were that simple. But it isn't! People are infinitely complex and so are their communications. For example, last night I heard my wife say, "Great!" I said, "What's 'great'?" She replied, "I can't find my letter opener anywhere and I just used it!" I thought "great" meant something wonderful had happened. She said "great" because she was irritated.

As you can see from the detailed model on the next page, communication is a very complicated process. Not only is there a sender, message, and receiver, there's also the situation or environment (when, where and how the communication occurs), and the feedback that one person receives as he or she talks and then listens to another.

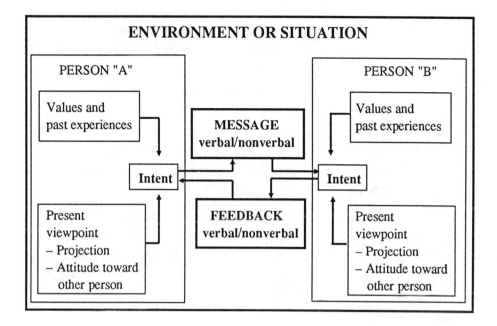

Using this model as a guide, we'll first look at the individuals involved in their communication with each other (values, past experiences, etc.), then the "message" itself, and last, the way feedback affects communication.

So let's look at each of these three elements in more detail.

The Sender and Receiver

The message someone sends depends on his or her intent, which in turn depends on the individual's values, past experience, present perceptions, attitude toward the other person, and language skills. And all of this depends on the situation (the environment) that surrounds the sender. That's a lot of "depends"!

Values and Past Experiences

To understand why some communication is not effective, you can look at your personal values. Values are those beliefs that are personally important to you in life. For example, I value my family over my work, but I value my work over other activities like watching TV or jogging. Values are strongly affected by the culture you grow up in—and by your age, sex, ethnic group, or race. Differences in age can be an especially important factor. For example, a woman I know went back to college after raising a family. She took some undergraduate level science courses (though she already had a master's degree in social work), then applied to medical school, and was accepted. She currently holds the unique honor of being the oldest female ever to graduate from her school.

But now, in a residency program at a local hospital, she finds it very difficult to maintain effective communication and working relationships with many of her fellow resident physicians. And her difficulty isn't due to her sex; many of the other residents are female. The problem lies mainly in the fact that she is in her late 40's, while most of her co-workers are in their 20's.

This age difference affects her ability to communicate in two ways. First, she has had considerable experience in life that her co-workers have not had: she has married, borne children, raised a family, worked in a variety of jobs, and experienced the death of a parent. For these reasons, she lacks commonality with most of her co-workers. If raising and relating to your children is one of the most important areas in your life, how much of this can you really share with those who have not yet had children? In short, this woman is simply at a different place in life than her professional peers—and she has greatly different interests.

But also, she grew up at a different time from that of her co-workers, and was taught a different set of work values. For example, she feels strongly that being a parent for her children has a higher priority than her career. Many of her co-workers feel just as strongly that becoming a physician has the highest priority. The resulting conflicts with some of her co-workers are natural. And they get in the way of effective communication with them.

This example illustrates that the closer you are in age to your co-workers, the more likely it is that you will have effective communications with them. But age difference is not the only cause of communications difficulty. Because our society still rewards boys (and later, men) for their interest and participation in sports, you more often see groups of men, rather than women, sitting around talking about last night's big game. Conversely, women have had unique sets of experiences that men haven't had, and these sex-related differences and interests can inhibit good communications with men.

Other differences—such as college vs. non-college experience, high vs. low income, and minority vs. non-minority status—can all interfere with effective communications. The fewer life experiences you have in common, the more different your values will be. And differing values tend to make communication more difficult.

When your values are not the same, it doesn't mean you can't communicate. But it does mean that communication requires special attention. When values are different, you have an even greater responsibility to follow good communication practices.

Having noted how important values and past experiences are in communicating, the next thing to examine is the sender's viewpoint as he or she communicates.

Present Perceptions

The sender of a message will often communicate from his or her own viewpoint rather than from that of the person to whom the message is sent. This occurs because of two major reasons: the projection of one person's feelings onto another, and the attitude of one person toward another person.

Projection. If I see my world as me, then I will tend to see others as extensions of me. If, for example, there is something that I fear, then I am apt to think that others will also have the same fear. And if they don't fear what I fear, then I am likely to think that there is something wrong with them.

Or, if there is a part of me that I don't like, then I am likely to expect to see that same thing in others. In other words, if I am secretly ashamed of a small part of me that is dishonest, I probably believe that others are also dishonest in the same way—even if they aren't.

Projections can create a lack of acceptance by one person for another, and thus cause communication problems. Let's look at an example. Bill, a new employee in the parts department of a large automotive company, was assigned to work with Joe, a senior employee. Joe was asked by the supervisor to help Bill learn the ropes. Joe was a perfectionist. During the first day, Joe spent a significant amount of time telling Bill what he was doing wrong, and did not mention any of the things that Bill did right. It's likely that Joe had some feelings inside about not being OK, and thus focused on the negatives of Bill's work rather than the positives. By the end of the day, Bill was feeling bad about himself, Joe, and the job. As a result, Bill withdrew and did not communicate with Joe, and didn't learn the job as quickly as he should have.

Attitude of one person for another. My attitude toward you will definitely affect the way I relate to you. If you and I have had trouble dealing with each other in the past, I am likely to have difficulty not only in speaking to you, but also in listening to you.

Let me give you a personal example. I once had an unpleasant experience with an individual who is a senior Human Resource Development specialist. But because of his expertise in proofing and editing, I put aside my negative feelings toward this person and asked him to be one of the reviewers of this book. Many of the comments that he wrote on the first draft of this book struck me as sarcastic and, even in some cases, cruel. But because his suggestions were excellent, I swallowed my pride (my initial reaction was to tell him where he could put his comments) and made the corrections that he offered. But I avoided any personal telephone calls to him even when, on several occasions, I should have called him to clarify a comment that I didn't understand.

However, as time went by, my original negative feeling lessened and I began to see his comments in a different light. Instead of sarcasm, I saw remarkable humor. Instead of cruelty, I saw an individual who could bluntly say what needed to be said about a piece of poor writing. Today, I am thankful that I asked him to be a reviewer, I am pleased that he said yes, and I deeply appreciate his contributions. You see, he didn't change—I did. And my change in attitude had a strong positive effect on our communication.

But I could have handled things better than I did. Rather than discovering that I felt better about him only as time went by, I could have taken the initiative and talked to him about my feelings. You see, the attitude we have toward another person is often a result of underlying feelings—feelings like mad, glad, sad. Powerful three- and four-letter words. Some people seem to be more inhibited about saying such words at work than the other kind of four-letter words. And yet, simply talking with others about your feelings can often reduce the intensity of your emotion.

So rather than deal directly with feelings, some people find it easier to use a distant "they" or "them," as in "I'm really unhappy about what *they* did!" or "I'm really mad at *them*!" What is much more difficult is, "I'm really mad at you!", "I am very unhappy over what you did!" or "I'm glad you are my friend." One solution is to express your mad/glad/sad feelings without using the word "you." You might feel more comfortable saying, "I am (state your feeling) because (state whatever happened or will happen)." For example, "I'm happy because we've been assigned to work together"; or, "I'm mad because I had to finish this job by myself even though we were both assigned to do it!"

We are not as direct as we should be for a number of reasons. Sometimes we are afraid. And when we are fearful, we may get angry.

So we develop "rituals" that protect us from others—or from ourselves. Here are some common types of rituals.

"Nothing." Example: Suppose that you and I are friends. A couple of days ago, I thought you were upset with me and I didn't know why. So I asked you what was wrong. You said, "Nothing." But I could tell by your expression that you were really upset. At this point, we have a serious communication problem. By saying "nothing," you get to stay mad, and I don't get an opportunity to try to resolve the problem. And if you stay angry in order to punish me for whatever I (or somebody else) did or didn't do, then we will continue to have a communication problem. In fact, the problem gets worse, because now I become upset. I'm angry at you for not leveling with me, and for not giving me a chance to explain my point of view, or to make amends—or simply to listen as your friend.

Kidding Around. Doug and Pete are good friends who avoid confronting each other over problems because they are afraid. They're afraid of what *might* happen to their relationship if they are direct with each other. So they use humor and kid around, in the hope that the other one will "get the message." The end result, however, is that one never knows exactly how the other feels—and thus is never really able to resolve problems that arise between them. Or there may be times when the other person gets the message and is hurt by it. The hurt creates anger which is suppressed in order to protect the relationship. This suppressed anger adds another weight to their relationship and may put a wall between them. Communication and trust will be diminished.

The Agreeables. Two co-workers are good friends. They work together and play together—but they don't fight together. So they often play a game called "Agreeable." It works like this: If they both want something, but only one can have it, they each try to persuade the other to take it. It is almost comical to watch them as one says, "Oh no, Bill, you take it." To which Bill responds, "Oh, I wouldn't dream of taking it, because I know how much you really want it."

Then Sam says, "What a wonderful friend you are! But there is no way that I could take it, since I know how important it is for *you* to have it!" To which Bill responds, "Well, Sam, that is very nice of you, but..."

Each has good reasons to want what he wants. But neither can ask directly for it. So they bend over backwards being "kind" and "considerate," depending on the other one to read their minds and satisfy their needs. As a result they may spend days trying not to make mistakes that will hurt their relationship.

Dancing. Have you ever watched two people "dance around" an issue because they are afraid to tackle it head on? Or maybe they're dancing because they don't know what really bothers them—so all they do is talk around the issue. The problem with dancing is that although it may be entertaining, it doesn't get anywhere. Here is a real-life example of a married couple we will name "Sandy" and "Jack," who finally stopped dancing around a serious issue.

Jack has a tough job which Sandy hates—with a passion. Last week, she again was bitterly complaining about the job's long hours (50 to 60 hours per week), the long drive (two hours per day), the stress and pressure, and the fact that Jack gets called out at all hours of the night to handle emergencies (a couple of times a week). Jack responded by saying, "I know all these things bother you. But what's really troubling you?" Suddenly, Sandy thought of her father, who had died from a heart attack, partially the result of a stressful job. She said, "I don't want you to die like my father did."

The true cause is now clear. They could move toward a solution based on the real cause of the problem—a fear of death. If Sandy sees Jack's job only as a problem of long commutes, then one solution is to move closer to the job. Or if she sees the problem as long hours, then a solution is to find another job; or to cut down the hours by hiring an assistant. But if the real cause of Sandy's distress is her fear of losing him, then they can look at solutions like, "Select the best ways to keep Jack healthy."

Rituals such as "nothing," "kidding around," the "agreeables," and "dancing" are poor—and finally destructive—substitutes for openly facing our problems with others. Direct communication of our feelings, done tactfully but without avoiding the issue, is almost always the best way to achieve good working relationships with others. Good communication results from honesty and believing in the ability of others to work constructively with us when they truly know how we feel.

At this point, the factors that affect the sender have been presented—factors like the person's values and past experience, and his or her present perceptions. Now we'll look at the message itself.

THE MESSAGE

What the other person hears you say (verbal message) and what he or she sees in your facial gestures (non-verbal message) must match. If they don't, guess which message carries the most weight? Right—the non-verbal message. You have probably heard all your life that what you do is much more believable than what you say. But nowhere is this more true than in one-on-one communications. In studies conducted with individuals who were sent mixed messages—i.e., where the non-verbal did not match the verbal—they were influenced 93% by non-verbal messages, and only 7% by verbal messages.

Non-Verbal Messages

Non-verbal messages can be lumped together into several major categories: eye contact, posture, facial expressions and gestures, and the quality of your voice. Let's look briefly at each of these.

Eye contact. Why do some people speak the truth yet look dishonest? Why can rascals lie and yet look absolutely believable? The answer is in their eyes!

Eyes are indeed the window of the soul. The soft gaze of the lover for his or her mate; the intense look that commands obedience; the eyes that smile at you as you talk; piercing, angry eyes—eyes are keys to your communication. And what your eyes communicate to others depends on:

1. how long you look;

2. where you look as you talk and listen; and

3. how long you blink your eyes.

How long you look. There is a big difference between staring eyes and darting eyes. The longer you look at a co-worker without looking away, the more you may be seen as intimidating. But if your eyes dart away from the other person and then back again, you could be seen as shifty. The common factor is time. In conversations with co-workers, the normal eye contact is somewhere between 5 and 10 seconds. A shorter look may cause you to appear sneaky to the other person. A longer look can result in the other person feeling threatened and uncomfortable.

Where you look as you talk and listen. If you look at the floor, walls, or ceiling as you communicate, you may appear to be disinterested in the conversation. If looking directly into someone's eyes makes you feel uncomfortable, try looking at some other part of the face. If you look at the other person's nose, chin, or forehead, you will still appear to be looking into his or her eyes.

How long you blink your eyes. Blinking your eyes is normal. But some people slowly shut their eyes as they talk or listen. This gives the impression that they are removing themselves from the conversation with the other person.

Posture. Notice your posture the next time you are in a one-on-one conversation. If you are standing, do you have your weight evenly balanced on both feet and are you leaning slightly forward? Or are you resting your weight on one leg and leaning away? If seated, are you leaning toward or away from the other person?

Of course, most people have privacy zones. Lovers, little children, and intimate friends are usually allowed closer than co-workers. If you stand too close or lean too far forward, they may feel uncomfortable. In this country, a distance of less than 18 inches is considered intimate. Private conversations with close friends usually take place from 18 to 24 inches, normal conversations with co-workers are usually 2 to 4 feet, and business conversations often take place at a distance of from 4 to 7 feet.

You can tell a lot about a relationship by observing how close people are to each other as they talk. For example, notice the difference in distance between you and your close friends compared to the distance between you and your boss. If your boss conducts participative performance appraisal reviews with you, he or she is likely to sit across the corner of his or her desk (2 to 4 feet). But if your boss is less participative in his or her management style, normal communication distance will usually be from 4 to 7 feet—i.e., across the desk rather than across the corner of the desk.

Facial expressions and gestures. There are a number of different facial expressions and gestures that can communicate, including smiling, frowning, yawning, and using the hands.

The smile. A genuine smile is a wonderful thing. It implies acceptance, caring, and friendship. When people are asked to place themselves into one of these three categories—seldom smiles, neutral expression, or often smiles—the great majority select often smiles. But when people are asked to rate others using the same scale, the average falls somewhere between seldom smiles and neutral. So something strange is going on. People obviously think they smile more than they really do.

The danger is that you may also think you smile often—but don't. If you are smiling on the inside but others see a neutral expression, then you are not communicating what you are really feeling. On the other hand, if you feel angry but are smiling, others will still get a mixed message. Your goal is to match what you say with what others see and with what you feel.

Frowning. A frown can communicate that you do not approve of what is being said, that you do not approve of the person with whom you are communicating, or that the situation that you are in is disagreeable. Part of the problem is that the person you are talking with may not be able to tell if you are frowning because of the message, because of him or herself, or because of the situation. For example, I often frown when I am writing. It isn't that I'm unhappy with what I am doing or even unhappy with others who may be around me—I am simply concentrating. Because a frown, like a smile, is often unconscious, you need to know when you frown so that others will see a message that matches what you say.

Using the hands. I use my hands when I talk. For example, when I listen to someone talk, and do not intend to interrupt, I will rest my chin on my hand. Or, if I want to let the other person know that I need to say something, I will often slightly raise my hand—almost an abbreviated version of a classroom response. If I want to demonstrate caring to another, I may touch him or her lightly on the arm or shoulder. I may even use my fingers to emphasize a point, as in, "There are three (holding up three fingers) areas to consider in looking at communication. First, (holding up my first finger) is the sender, second (holding up another finger) the message, and third (holding up three fingers) the receiver." But I try very hard not to point my finger at another as I talk, because this may appear parental. And I also try not to tap my finger or a pencil on the desk as I am talking, because the other person may feel that I don't have time for him or her.

Quality of your voice. The two major factors that affect the quality of your voice are tone and pace. Your tone is a function of voice frequency, resonance, and loudness. Pace is related to the speed at which you talk as well as your use of pauses.

Voice tone. Without training, it is difficult to change the resonance of your voice. But you can change the frequency and loudness of your normal speaking voice. It is possible, with practice, to change your natural frequency either up or down. If you feel that your voice is pitched too high, you can deliberately lower the frequency. Or, if it is too low, you can raise it. If you speak too loudly or softly, you can also develop the habit of speaking at a more appropriate level.

Pace. This is the one that gets me in trouble. I'm OK until I get excited—then I talk too fast. Like most things, it is a habit. But over the years, I have been fairly successful in slowing down even when my mind is racing.

Pausing appropriately can also enhance the quality of your speech. Not only does it give you a chance to think more about what you are going to say, it also makes it easier for your listener to understand what you are saying. But it is also possible to overdo the pause. In this country, if you pause too long, the other person will feel the need to speak. So you need to find a balance—pausing often enough to improve the quality of your speech and at the same time not pausing so long that the other person begins to feel uncomfortable.

Verbal Messages

By verbal, I mean the words that you use, the meaning that others give to your words, speech habits, and the use of questions. Let's look at each of these.

Jargon, technical language, abbreviations or acronyms. When words are unfamiliar to your receiver, or abstract in their meaning, then the probability of a communication problem is increased. When jargon, technical language, abbreviations, or acronyms (letters selected to represent a compound word or a series of words—e.g., "TNT" is an acronym for Trinitrotoluene) are used with others who are not familiar with them, communication is much more difficult. In my field, for example, everybody knows what an "HRD" specialist is. But since most of my readers are not HRD specialists, I did not use HRD earlier, but spelled it out as Human Resource Development.

There is nothing inherently wrong with jargon, technical language, abbreviations, or acronyms—they can save time and help you communicate more precisely to others who are in the same job or profession. But the use of jargon or overly technical language with people who don't have the foggiest idea what you're talking about is definitely poor communication.

The meaning of words. Words don't have meanings. People assign meaning to words. Meanings are assigned based on your own experience. If your experiences are different from mine, then it is likely that your meanings may also be different. For example, in this chapter I have used the word "value" thirteen times. Yet, any dictionary will give a variety of definitions such as:

1. The worth of something in money.

2. The purchasing power of the dollar.

3. What you desire or hold important in life.

4. What society sees as important.

5. The worth of a particular playing card.

When I used the word "value" in the original rough draft of this chapter, I did not define it. Later, in editing it, one of the reviewers wrote, "I have some concern that your audience will not clearly understand what you mean by 'values.'" So in the rewrite, I defined the word by saying, "Values are those beliefs that are personally important to you in life." Note too that I didn't just write the word "acronym" in the beginning of this section, but also defined it as "letters selected to represent a compound word or a series of words."

Speech habits. There are people who end nearly every sentence with, "OK?", "Right?" or "You know?" Or they start every sentence with "I guess..." If you have a speech habit like any of these, realize that it drives some people nuts. Your listeners can become so conscious of your use of a particular word that they will stop hearing what you're saying.

At this point, you have seen how communication can be affected by the sender's and the receiver's values and past experiences, their present viewpoints as a result of projections and attitudes, and the non-verbal and verbal parts of the message. The last step is to look at the feedback that the sender gets from the receiver, or vice versa.

FEEDBACK

Feedback occurs not only when you stop talking and begin to listen to another; it also happens even as you talk. You are certainly aware of the other person's expressions, for example, frowns or smiles—as well as other non-verbal gestures like nodding. These signals can tell you when your message is being received and even to some extent, if you are being understood.

But for the most part, communication without verbal feedback is nothing more than a presentation. If you really want to talk with rather than at someone, then you've got to listen to what the other person has to say.

Non-Verbal Feedback

Listen without interrupting. This basic rule of communication and courtesy is often violated. In conversation, you may become so interested in what you want to say next, that you don't really listen to what the other person is saying. Since you can speak at a rate of about 150 words per minute but can listen at well over 750, you are going to have a lot of extra time while someone else is talking. This is both a curse and a blessing. It's a curse because as someone else speaks, your thoughts are likely to be going in a dozen different directions. And if you chase down an interesting thought, you may lose track of what the other person is saying. But it's a blessing because the extra time can give you a chance to really concentrate on the other person, focusing on what he or she is saying, and trying to understand the message in light of your own past experience.

Nodding. You can encourage verbal feedback by nodding as the other person talks. There was an interesting study that demonstrated that one nod increased the flow of communication, two nods neither increased nor decreased communication, and three or more nods in rapid succession decreased communication. These results do seem to fit with my experience. Single nods appropriately spaced certainly do encourage others to continue to talk. And I have known people who nodded so much and so often that it was distracting.

Posture. Your posture while listening to another person is called "attending." You attend to other people while talking or listening when your body communicates that you are interested in being with them. If you are standing, balance your weight on both feet and lean slightly forward. If you are seated, just lean forward. This is attending.

Of course, there are individuals who will talk your ears off if you let them. With people like this, a well-timed interruption is appropriate. But really listening to what someone else is saying is beneficial, for several reasons. First, it will help you gain more information; and in general, the more information you have, the better will be your response. Second, listening is very complimentary—we all like to be listened to! Finally, sometimes people don't want, or need, a response. They just want someone to listen.

Verbal Feedback

There are a number of ways you can verbally encourage the other person to give you feedback. You can reflect what someone is saying or feeling, you can ask questions, and you can summarize.

Reflecting. To obtain more information, or feedback, you can simply restate what the other person has said and ask if what you heard was correct. Or you can state the feelings that you saw in the other person and again ask if what you saw was correct. Either way works—by encouraging the other person to continue to talk.

For example, suppose that you and I were not only co-workers, but also car-pooled together. One day while on break you said, "Dick, maybe if your work area weren't quite so messy, it wouldn't take us so long to get out of here at the end of the day." Somewhat irritated I replied, "Well if you weren't such a perfectionist, and could live with a little more normal disorder in your life, then it wouldn't be a problem for you!"

At this point, you have two ways of reflecting my statement. You could focus on the facts by saying, "You see me as a perfectionist and think that your desk is normal, is that correct?" Then stay silent, and I will probably respond. On the other hand, you could reflect my feelings by saying, "You seem irritated that I see your work area as messy, is that right?" Again, keep your mouth closed and wait for my response.

Asking questions. Asking good questions is an excellent way of obtaining feedback from the other person. For example, if you made a comment about your job to a co-worker and she responded by saying, "Boy, do I hate my job!", you might respond by telling her all the things you, too, don't like about your job. But a better communication strategy would be to ask, "What is it about the job that bothers you the most?" Then, listen as she tells you!

Open questions. Note the use of an "open" question—the one that began with the word "What"—in the above example. Open questions begin with the words, "What, How, When, Where, Who, Which or Why." They are used to gain more information, and cannot usually be answered with just "Yes" or "No."

Open questions that yield the most information usually start with "What" or "How." Other open questions, beginning with "When" or "Where," can also help you understand the other person, since they obtain more specific details; but they are also less useful for acquiring general information. The least desirable question seems to be the personal "Why" question—as in, "Why do you hate this job?" If your coworker is a good friend, this question is probably OK. But if not, a "Why" combined with "you" can produce defensive behavior, since the question focuses on personal motives.

Closed questions. "Closed" questions, on the other hand, are those that are used to direct or guide discussions—and are normally answered with a "Yes" or "No." For example, "Do you...?", "Have you...?", "Are you...?", "Would you...?", "Can you...?", and "Should you...?" are closed questions. Some questions in this category are perceived as requests for more information; but technically they are "closed" questions. For instance, questions like, "Can you be more specific?" or "Could you give me an example?" are not normally answered with a "Yes" or "No," even though they are in fact closed questions. Thus they are good questions to use in obtaining feedback from the other person.

Guided questions. Another way to enhance communication is to use "guided" questions. Guided questions direct the discussion to either the positive or negative side of an issue. For example, if your co-worker responded to you by saying, "I really like my job, but my family hates it," you can guide the discussion to either side of this statement by asking:

"What do you like about your job?" (positive)
"How does your job affect your family?" (negative)

Loaded Questions. When asking or answering questions, carefully avoid what are termed "loaded" questions. Suppose you made a comment about your boss, Carol. Your co-worker responds by saying, "Don't you think that Carol is a jerk?" Your co-worker did not really ask a "question." He or she actually stated an *opinion* in the form of a question. Questions like, "Don't you think...?", "Don't you feel...?", or "Wouldn't you agree that...?" are really just expressions of the speaker's strong opinion. People often mask opinions as questions because they feel it is "safer" than saying openly, "I believe that...!" If you want to find out what someone else believes or feels, you should ask them directly. And if you have an opinion about something that you want to express, then you should be equally direct, and express that opinion without putting it in the form of a "loaded" question.

Summarizing. Summarizing what you heard the other person say is a powerful communication tool for the following reasons:

1. It will help ensure that what you heard is what the other person really said.

2. It will force you to listen better.

3. It will improve your retention.

4. If you keep quiet after your summary, the other person will probably give you additional information.

You don't need a tape recorder to summarize what the other person said. Just listen intently, and when the other person is finished speaking, simply summarize the highlights of what you heard.

As we have seen, one-on-one communications is not simple at all—it is quite complex. I hope that you have gained additional insight into the process of communication by reading about the sender and receiver, the message, and the need to obtain feedback about what was said. The following pages are designed to help you put into practice the concepts presented in this chapter.

COMMUNICATION ANALYSIS
PART 1

This work sheet is designed to be used to help you develop your communication skills. It will show you how to plan a communication session with another person, and will help you critique yourself afterwards.

If additional work sheets are needed, please copy these pages.

Name of person you will be interviewing: _____

1. **CONSIDER YOUR SIMILARITIES AND DIFFERENCES IN BACKGROUND**

Indicate sex: You _____   The other person _____

Age:
Big difference ____   Somewhat different ____   No difference ____

Education:
Big difference ____   Somewhat different ____   No difference ____

Income:
Big difference ____   Somewhat different ____   No difference ____

Race: Different _____   Same _____

How might differences get in the way of my communication with this other person?

_____
_____
_____

2. POSSIBLE PROJECTIONS

What, if anything, don't I like about this person that I also don't like in myself? _____

_____

_____

Could this be a projection of my own imagination onto the other person, or is he or she really this way? _____

What, if anything, irritates or concerns me about this person that might get in the way of our communication?   _____

_____

_____

Again, could this be a projection of my own feelings? _____

3. ATTITUDES

What problems have I had in the past with this person that influences my feelings toward him or her? _____

_____

_____

What can I do about any unresolved problems that may exist?

_____

_____

What, if any, "games" do we play? (e.g., "Nothing," "Kidding Around," "The Agreeables," or "Dancing.")

_____

_____

After completing this section of your communication analysis, schedule a private interview with this person to discuss your answers and resolve any differences in opinions, if possible.

COMMUNICATION ANALYSIS
PART 2

When you have finished discussing Part 1, ask the other person to give you honest feedback on the following questions.

1. NON-VERBAL MESSAGES

Eye contact

• My length of eye contact is:

Too long _____   Just right _____   Too short _____

• Where do I look when I talk to you? _____

_____

• Do I shut my eyes too long as I communicate with you? _____

Facial expressions and gestures

• How often do I smile?

Not enough _____   OK _____   Too much _____

• How often do I frown?

Not enough _____   OK _____   Too much _____

• How much do I use my hands when I talk?

OK _____   Not OK _____

If "Not OK," how could I improve? _____

_____

_____

_____

2. VERBAL MESSAGES

Quality of my voice

• How is the pitch (frequency) of my voice?
   Too low _____   Just right _____   Too high _____

• How is the loudness of my voice?
   Too soft _____   Just right _____   Too loud _____

• Do I pause appropriately?   Yes _____   No _____

• How well do I balance the time I talk with the time I listen?
   Don't talk   Good   Talk too
   enough _____   balance _____   much _____

Jargon, technical language, abbreviations, or acronyms.

• Do I use jargon, technical language, abbreviations, or acronyms
   when I communicate?   Yes _____   No _____

   If so, what kind of problems does this cause in my communication? _____ _____
   _____
   _____
   _____

• How well do I use words to communicate?
   Need improvement _____   OK _____
   If my vocabulary needs improving, how should I improve it?
   _____
   _____
   _____

• Do I have any speech habits that interfere with communication?
   No _____   Yes _____   If so, what? _____
   _____
   _____

3. FEEDBACK

Non-verbal feedback

- How often do you feel that I interrupt you when we are talking?
  Seldom _____   Often _____

- Do I nod my head appropriately as I listen to you?
  Seldom _____   OK _____   Too much nodding _____

- How would you judge my posture? In other words, do I look like I am really listening to you as you talk? _____
  _____
  _____

Verbal feedback

- How well do I reflect to you what I thought I heard you say?
  _____
  _____
  _____

- How well do I use questions to find out more about how you feel about the topic under discussion? _____
  _____
  _____

- How well do I summarize what you have said in a conversation?
  _____
  _____
  _____

When the interview is over, consider in private the conversation you had. Note below the key points you learned about yourself.

_____
_____
_____
_____
_____
_____
_____
_____
_____
_____
_____
_____
_____

As a result of what you have learned, what are you going to do to further improve your communication skills? _____

_____
_____
_____
_____
_____
_____
_____
_____
_____
_____
_____
_____
_____

When the interview is over, consider... review the conversation you had. Note below the key points you learned about yourself.

_____

_____

_____

_____

_____

_____

_____

_____

_____

_____

_____

_____

_____

Based on what you have learned, what are you going to do to... for your communication?

_____

_____

_____

_____

_____

_____

_____

_____

_____

_____

_____

_____

CHAPTER 4
WORKING EFFECTIVELY
WITH OTHERS

If you stop to consider people you would enjoy working with, it's often fairly easy to think of some names. It is also easy to think of people you would definitely *not* want to work with! But did you ever wonder why? Why do some people seem desirable as work partners, and others appear undesirable?

Consider those individuals you would enjoy working with by thinking of short "descriptors" of them. Words and phrases may quickly come to mind—like:

Friendly	Does his or her share and more
Doesn't take all the credit	Hard working
Loyal	Does what he says he's going
Doesn't complain	to do
Not bossy	Has good work habits
Easygoing	Talks with me
Honest with me and others	Serious about his or her job
Has good ideas	Doesn't get sidetracked
Not critical	Helpful

Sometimes what seems like a strength can also cause trouble. For example, someone could see us as non-critical (a strength). But this characteristic might cause us to have difficulty giving constructive feedback to an individual when it is justified, and even desired. Or the strength "talks with me" can cause a problem if the individual talks too much. In fact, we can create a continuum concerning almost any of the descriptors above. For example:

```
x ————————————— x ————————————— x
Silent and              Talks              Talks too
withdrawn            appropriately            much
```

The secret of working with people is to avoid the extremes. But unfortunately, we don't always know where we are on the continuum, probably because we don't see ourselves as clearly as others do.

Two psychologists, Joseph Luft and Harry Ingham, developed a model that can help us better understand ourselves. Their model, called the "Johari Window," looks like an old fashioned window with four panes of glass.

1. What I know about me. What others know about me.	2. What I know about me. What others don't know about me.
3. What I don't know about about me. What others know about me.	4. What I don't know about me. What others don't know about me.

Block #1 contains all those things that I am aware of, and that others also know. For example, I am very much aware that I can't spell, and my co-workers also know this about me.

In Block #2 are those things that I am aware of but don't choose to tell anyone else. An example of this happened in a class I once took. Our instructor told a joke that clearly demonstrated his prejudice toward blacks. His assumption was that we were all "good ol' boys" and would find his so-called joke funny. It wasn't funny to me. In fact, I was offended that he thought that I would find it humorous. At that moment, I was very much aware of my feelings—he was not.

Suppose we consider my instructor the "I" (the subject) in the Johari Window illustration. Being unaware of his impact on others (me, in this case), he would be in Block #3. That is, he knew that he used ethnic humor, but wasn't aware of its impact on others.

At the end of the class, I asked him if he would like some private feedback. When he said yes, I told him how I had felt about the "joke." It was to his credit that he accepted the feedback graciously and changed his behavior in the future. By being open for feedback, he moved from Block #3 to Block #1, thus increasing his self-knowledge.

The things in Block #4 are usually those things that are said to be in the subconscious. For example, an individual who had an emotionally abusing childhood may unconsciously keep others at a distance and not have close friends in order to keep from being "hurt." In this case, the person is probably not even aware that he or she doesn't allow others to become emotionally close. At the same time, co-workers are also unaware that they are being kept at a distance.

Because they are afraid of hurting someone else's feelings, people are reluctant to give others feedback. But without feedback, how can we learn about those things that others see, but we don't?

Part of the answer is to find a way to ask others for feedback. One way is to copy the following pages describing how others see you and then to ask some trusted friends to fill them out. While you are waiting for their responses, fill out the same pages in terms of how you see yourself. Then, compare how your friends saw you with how you saw yourself.

You may find it easier to ask several people to complete this form anonymously. Friends may feel more comfortable, and be more truthful, if asked to fill out the survey anonymously.

WORKING EFFECTIVELY WITH OTHERS

Name of the person being
reviewed: _____

Name of the person filling
out this form: _____

Date: _____

By putting an "X" in the appropriate box, please indicate below your opinion of me in each of 16 areas. I've asked you to complete this review because you are my friend. True friends give honest feedback. Therefore, be as honest as possible in your review.

In my work with others, how do you rate me on the following:

1. Friendliness:

0	1	2	3	4	5	4	3	2	1	0

Unfriendly   Friendly   Excessively
                                                          friendly

2. Giving credit for work done with others:

0	1	2	3	4	5	4	3	2	1	0

Takes all   Gives credit   Cannot take
the credit   when due   credit

3. Loyalty:

0	1	2	3	4	5	4	3	2	1	0

Disloyal   Loyal   Blindly
                                                         supportive

4. Expressing complaints:

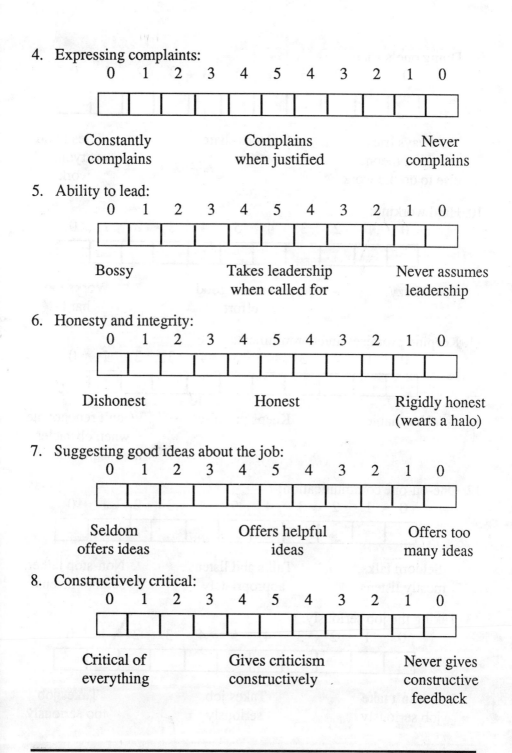

| 0 | 1 | 2 | 3 | 4 | 5 | 4 | 3 | 2 | 1 | 0 |

Constantly
complains

Complains
when justified

Never
complains

5. Ability to lead:

| 0 | 1 | 2 | 3 | 4 | 5 | 4 | 3 | 2 | 1 | 0 |

Bossy

Takes leadership
when called for

Never assumes
leadership

6. Honesty and integrity:

| 0 | 1 | 2 | 3 | 4 | 5 | 4 | 3 | 2 | 1 | 0 |

Dishonest

Honest

Rigidly honest
(wears a halo)

7. Suggesting good ideas about the job:

| 0 | 1 | 2 | 3 | 4 | 5 | 4 | 3 | 2 | 1 | 0 |

Seldom
offers ideas

Offers helpful
ideas

Offers too
many ideas

8. Constructively critical:

| 0 | 1 | 2 | 3 | 4 | 5 | 4 | 3 | 2 | 1 | 0 |

Critical of
everything

Gives criticism
constructively

Never gives
constructive
feedback

9. Doing one's share:

| 0 | 1 | 2 | 3 | 4 | 5 | 4 | 3 | 2 | 1 | 0 |

Always tries to get someone else to do the work

Does share

Tries to do everyone's work

10. Hard working:

| 0 | 1 | 2 | 3 | 4 | 5 | 4 | 3 | 2 | 1 | 0 |

Lazy

Makes a good effort

Works too hard

11. Keeping promises and commitments:

| 0 | 1 | 2 | 3 | 4 | 5 | 4 | 3 | 2 | 1 | 0 |

Unreliable

Keeps promises

Can't renegotiate when obstacles are insurmountable

12. One-on-one communication:

| 0 | 1 | 2 | 3 | 4 | 5 | 4 | 3 | 2 | 1 | 0 |

Seldom talks, mostly listens

Talks and listens appropriately

Non-stop talker, seldom listens

13. Taking the job seriously:

| 0 | 1 | 2 | 3 | 4 | 5 | 4 | 3 | 2 | 1 | 0 |

Doesn't take job seriously

Takes job seriously

Takes job too seriously

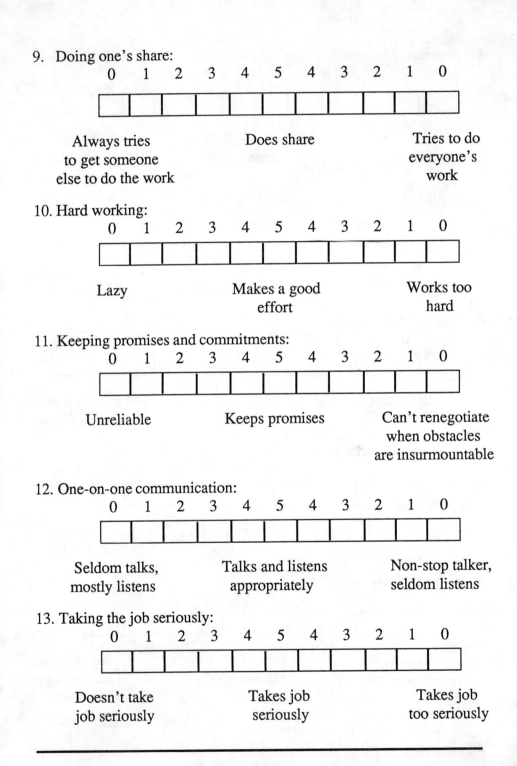

14. Good work habits (clean area, not tardy, follows safety procedures, doesn't take time off when not sick, etc.):

0   1   2   3   4   5   4   3   2   1   0

Poor work habits   Good work   Compulsive
                            habits   work habits

15. Giving praise when deserved:

0   1   2   3   4   5   4   3   2   1   0

Never praises   Gives deserved   Overpraises
                           praise   (flattery)

16. Helpfulness:

0   1   2   3   4   5   4   3   2   1   0

Never helps   Helps others   Tries to be
                     appropriately   too helpful

After completing the evaluation(s), record the scores for each description below:

	Friend "A"	Friend "B"	Friend "C"	Friend "D"	Your Self Rating
1. Friendliness	___	___	___	___	___
2. Giving the credit for work done	___	___	___	___	___
3. Loyalty	___	___	___	___	___
4. Expressing complaints when appropriate	___	___	___	___	___
5. Ablity to lead	___	___	___	___	___
6. Honest	___	___	___	___	___
7. Suggesting good ideas about the job	___	___	___	___	___
8. Constructively critical	___	___	___	___	___
9. Doing one's share	___	___	___	___	___
10. Hard working	___	___	___	___	___
11. Keeping promises and commitments	___	___	___	___	___
12. One-on-one communication	___	___	___	___	___
13. Taking the job seriously	___	___	___	___	___
14. Good work habits	___	___	___	___	___
15. Giving praise when deserved	___	___	___	___	___
16. Helpfulness	___	___	___	___	___
Subtotals	___	___	___	___	___

Total points ("A" + "B" + "C" + "D") ____

Average # of points (Total # points divided by # of reviewers)____

After receiving and recording the completed reviews from your friends, look carefully at their ratings. Then compare their ratings with your own self-review. Note areas where your raters do not perceive you as you view yourself. Realizing that others see you differently from the way you see yourself, and examining why, is an important step in better understanding yourself and your way of relating.

Finally—and most important—note those ratings that are less than 2 (i.e., 0 and 1 ratings). These ratings (on either side of 5) indicate the extremes of positive traits, and might suggest areas that need improvement in your relationship with that person on the job.

If you have areas where your own self-perception differs greatly from your raters' view of you, or areas where your ratings are less than 2 (suggesting imbalances), arrange to meet privately with your raters to discuss these areas. Even if your survey was conducted anonymously, you can still conduct follow-up interviews and ask your friends if they concur with the feedback. If so, ask them for specific examples of why they perceive you as they do in these areas. Then you will be in a position to decide whether you need to change your style of working, and working with others.

As an example of this process, say that several of my friends evaluate me less than 2 in the category of "Hard working," as too hard working. My first task is to talk with each of them and ask for examples of their perception. Then I am in a better position to make decisions about whether or not I want to change. I may decide that I like being seen as "working too hard." But the fact that I "work too hard" may also cause problems for others. For example, others who must process my work may begin to feel overloaded with my output.

If you decide that you need to do something about a specific area, the next job is to develop a plan for change. Here again, your friends can be a great help in providing ideas to include in your plan.

And one word of caution: Don't overwhelm yourself trying to change in too many areas at once. There is plenty of time to make important changes in your way of relating to others and the job. Simply ask yourself, "What are the three most important things I want to change today?"—and do it consistently!

Change may not be easy. But it is possible! It first takes a clear understanding of what needs to be changed, then a willingness to do so. But it is also nice to have support while you are making important and significant changes. So if you have a close friend, spouse, or confidant, you may wish to ask him or her to help see you through each stage of your change. One thing is certain—the results will be very rewarding to you and others!

On the next page is an interview and planning form which you can use to obtain additional information from your friends.

INTERVIEW FORM
WORKING EFFECTIVELY WITH OTHERS

1. Area(s) of improvement that I need to investigate:

_____

_____

_____

2. Friend(s), or others, I want to interview.

_____   _____

_____   _____

_____   _____

INTERVIEW(S)

3. Examples and/or illustrations of area(s) of concern:

_____

_____

_____

_____

_____

_____

4. Answers to the question, "How does this have a negative impact on my performance, or on our relationship?"

_____

_____

_____

_____

_____

5. Ideas on what I can do about this situation if I decide that change is beneficial:

_____
_____
_____
_____
_____
_____
_____

CHAPTER 5
HOW TO RECEIVE WORK
ASSIGNMENTS

Suppose your boss has just asked you to complete a task, but you don't have the foggiest idea how to do it. At this point you can:

1. Ask questions to find out more about the task.

2. Say, "I don't know how to do that job."

3. Say, "That's not *my* job."

4. Ignore the assignment.

Which of the four responses is the most responsible?

Number one—"ask questions" is probably the best response. Number two is a passive response; and number three is hostile. Actually, responses two and three are very similar. They both communicate to the boss that you don't want to do the job. And answer number four is a potential disaster, not only for you, but also for your boss and co-workers. When assigned work is ignored, it can cause serious hardship for others who depend on you.

A key step in becoming an effective employee is to accept responsibility. Success starts with you! If you are assigned a task that you don't know how to do, ask questions. "What exactly do you want me to do?" "Where can I go to find out how it ought to be done?" "How do you want me to proceed?" "Is there a specific sequence that would be more effective in completing this task?"

For more complicated assignments, ask your supervisor to help you write out a step-by-step procedure. Start out by asking what the end result of the task should look like. Then ask your boss if he or she has any preference in how the task can best be accomplished. Take notes and then read them back to your supervisor to help ensure understanding of the assignment. During this phase of the discussion, you can also offer ideas on how to improve the quality of the job. These comments will communicate to your supervisor that you understand what is being discussed.

The amount of information you need depends a lot on what you already know about the assigned task—and your boss's delegation style. The more you already know about the task, the fewer questions you may need to ask. If your boss has a delegation style that encourages you to take responsibility for the details of the plan, you may choose to ask only questions that define the general outlines of the job, not the specific details. In this case, a better approach is to receive the assignment and determine any needed deadlines, sketch out in private a general plan of attack, and then discuss the plan with your boss. If you're lucky enough to work for a supervisor who will allow you to take the initiative, then take it!

Another way of better visualizing a new task is to ask questions about how it is like—or not like—an old task. Also, you can ask for an example, illustration, or a demonstration.

Misunderstandings occur when both the supervisor and the employee think there is mutual understanding of what was said—and there wasn't. So don't be afraid to repeat your questions if you are not sure you understand what was said. And when you receive an answer to a question you can repeat, in your own words, what you thought you heard, and ask if that is correct. You will be amazed at the number of times your supervisor will say, "No, not exactly. What I said was..."

You can even ask "Why?" questions—tactfully. Even though the days of "Because I said so!" are mostly gone, a why question can still sound challenging unless it is well-phrased. A simple "Why is it important that this be done?" is usually less threatening to your supervisor than, "Why do I have to do this?" If you can determine the reasons why something needs to be done, they will help you greatly in carrying out the task. "Why" answers will often make it easier to understand the importance of the new task. They will also help you do the best thing, or make the right decisions, if things don't go exactly as planned.

It is also important for you to clearly know what the final results of your work should be. In other words, what is a "good" job? Or, what should the job or task look like when you have finished it? These questions are important because 1) they allow you to measure your own performance; and 2) they will help you know when you have completed the task assignment.

You can also ask your supervisor when he or she will be available for additional questions. It can be very frustrating to be two hours into a new task and suddenly discover the need for additional information—only to find that your boss is out of the office for the rest of the afternoon.

The most important thing is to *ask questions!* Good questions are—

Questions to the Boss	Questions to Myself
"When do you want me to start?"	What am I now doing that may interfere with this new task?
"When should the job be completed?"	Are other activities already scheduled that would interfere with the deadline?
"Where can I go to find out how it ought to be done?"	What don't I know that I need to know to complete this task?
"What potential problems do you see?"	What potential problems do I see?
"What other people should I see about this?"	Who else is likely to be involved in this? Are they people that I can easily talk with?
"How often do you want feedback on my progress?"	How hard is it going to be for me to tell the boss if things don't go well? If I find that I need to do things a little differently, how much does the boss need to know? How approachable is my boss?
"What does good performance on this job look like?"	How will I know when I've done a good job? What is going to happen if I screw this up?

These questions appear on a "Check Sheet" found on the next page. This page can be reproduced by you and used to help you in receiving work assignments.

CHECK SHEET
HOW TO RECEIVE WORK ASSIGNMENTS

1. Why is it important that this be done?

   _____
   _____
   _____

2. When do you want me to begin? _____

3. When should the job be completed? _____

4. Where can I go to find out how it ought to be done?

   _____
   _____
   _____

5. What potential problems do you see?

   _____
   _____
   _____

6. What potential problems do I see?

   _____
   _____
   _____

7. Whom else should I see? _____

8. How often do you want feedback on my progress?

   _____

   _____

   _____

9. What does a "good" job look like?

   _____

   _____

   _____

10. When will you be available if I have additional questions? Whom should I consult if you are unavailable?

   _____

CHAPTER 6
HOW TO SOLVE PROBLEMS

Some people seem to have a knack for coming up with the best solution to a problem. Others with the same intelligence and experience seem to come up with solutions before they are even sure what the problems are! We've all seen examples of disasters that occurred when the cause of the problem wasn't analyzed before expensive action was taken: decisions made that resulted in wasted time, materials and money; plans that looked perfect on paper, but failed in real life.

This chapter will help you develop skills in problem solving. It will show you logical—and simple—ways to make your problem-solving effective.

A key step emphasized in this chapter is writing out the problem! It is amazing what a simple thing like writing down information can do to increase your success in solving problems. You don't always have a clipboard in your hand, but, whenever you have a problem, begin by taking a minute to make the problem "visible" in writing.

Visibility does several things:

- First, if a problem-solving process is taking place only in your mind, no one can help you. Others are kept from pointing out oversights, errors, or faulty assumptions.

- Second, if you do not make your thinking visible, you do not have a reliable way to review how you attempted to solve a problem and therefore to learn from your past mistakes.

- Third, writing the problem down will help you see the whole problem, rather than just unorganized parts and pieces.

SITUATION ANALYSIS

"Situation Analysis" (S.A.) is a problem solving tool that will help you break a large, even messy, situation down into manageable pieces. These pieces become the problems, decisions, plans, or even the new problem situations to be analyzed. So when you have a problem that is big, complex, bulky, and has lots of parts and pieces, this is probably the time for S.A. Problems like "I'm unhappy on the job," "I don't get along with my boss," or "I have trouble at home" are often called problems. Technically they are not problems at all, but statements about symptoms of problems. And for concerns like these, a good tool to reach for is Situation Analysis.

Let's take a messy situation, and see how S.A. can be used to break it down.

THE CASE OF THE UNHAPPY EMPLOYEE

My name is Rick. I am employed by the American Data Corporation headquartered in Atlanta, Georgia. I'm married, have two children, a fairly large dog (Golden Retriever), and a cat of unknown origin that was left on our doorstep a couple of years ago. I drive about 30 miles to my job (it takes me about 45 minutes), and so I spend about an hour and a half in the car every day. The traffic is getting worse. More cars, trucks and buses! Sometimes I wonder if the world will end up as one huge parking lot.

Speaking of parking—what a hassle! If I park on the street, my car gets towed and I get a ticket, or I lose my hubcaps. Two weeks ago my car got towed, I got a parking ticket, *and* two of my hubcaps were stolen. Lately, I've been keeping my car in a parking deck. The cost is horrible (but hubcaps are even more expensive; I paid $156 plus tax for the two hubcaps!).

We just got a new medical plan at the company. Ugh! They used to pay 100% of the cost. It took care of eyeglasses, dental work, and visits to our family doctor. This new plan not only restricts us to their list of approved doctors (our doctor is not on the list); I now have to pay half of the monthly premium.

My boss is having serious trouble with her marriage. I know how difficult this must be for her. But I wish she could leave her problems at home. I know she can't, but I still wish she would. Because she's irritable and withdrawn, it's really hard to be around her. It's been months since she has given anybody a pat on the back. She is so miserable with her own problems that she doesn't have time for us anymore. In fact, it seems to me that she resents it when we do need her for something.

But I guess what bothers me most is that I was passed over for promotion. I was given some kind of story about how the other person was better qualified. I don't believe it. I know the other person, and she is not better qualified. The only reason why she got promoted over me is that she's a "she"! I know that our EEO numbers are in trouble. But why are they penalizing me for what they did years ago? It just isn't fair. With all the expenses I have, I could sure use the extra money.

Money is tight. I just took Gladys (our dog, not my wife) to the vet for a skin rash. Wow, have you paid a vet bill lately? 120 bucks! I had to put it on my charge card. And Betty, my wife, wants to quit her job and find part-time employment so she can go back to college. That's nice—but how are we going to pay for it?

My car just turned over 100,000 miles. It was fun watching all those zeros come up. But what isn't fun is that the water pump needs replacing—again! This will be the third time that I've replaced the water pump on that car. And talk about money. It used to be that if you spent $100 in a garage, you had something major fixed. Now, 100 bucks won't even pay for a rebuilt water pump!

I have this fantasy. One morning I drive to work, but I don't stop. I slide onto Interstate 20 and head west. The sun is at my back, and the open road is ahead. I'm free. No worries, no responsibilities! I stop for lunch in Tuscaloosa, have supper in Jackson, and watch the sun set over the Mississippi. Then I rent a bateau in Vicksburg—and float down the river to New Orleans. Just call me "Huck"! I'm usually an optimistic kind of individual. But things are not going well. Maybe what I need is to start looking for another job. I've got 11 years with the company—but I don't think I can put up with much more.

Step 1. Write down the problem

The first step in using Situation Analysis is to make the problem statement visible. ***Write it down!***

Step 2. Separate the problem into its related parts

Separating out the pieces allows you to focus your energy on those areas that most affect the initial problem—and at the same time to see the problem as a whole. At this point, you don't have to analyze or conclude anything. Just jot down as many parts and pieces of the problem as you can think of. In our example, Rick would ask himself the question: "What are the things that make me say, 'I'm unhappy'?"

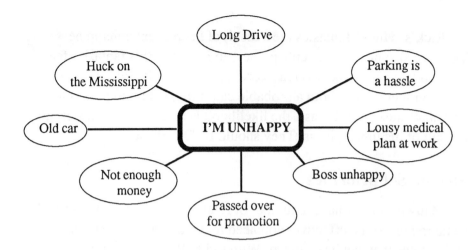

Step 3. Determine which pieces are probable causes and which are probable results

In this step, decide which of the separate pieces are causes, and which are *results* of causes. To fix a mess you must attack the causes, not the results. This is why your first step is to determine the probable causes.

Indicate a probable cause by drawing an arrow pointing to the problem situation, and a probable result with an arrow pointing away from the problem. Then cross out the results, and focus your energies on the causes. Here's an example:

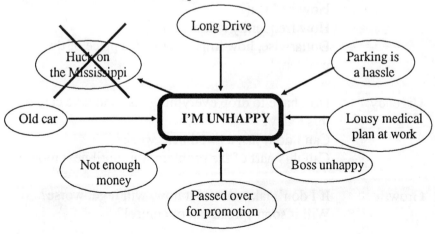

Rick's "Huck" fantasies are a result of his present unhappiness. They are also causing his unhappiness to intensify (his fantasies feel so good that they make his real world feel worse). If a piece of the situation seems to be both a probable cause *and* result, treat it as a probable cause. In this case, the likelihood is that Rick's fantasies are a result of his unhappiness. They should be "X'ed" out.

Step 4. Set priorities

Many problems have a number of related causes, some major and some minor. To be effective, you need to devote your time to the major areas that can be changed. With tight schedules, you just don't have time to do everything. Therefore, fix the things that matter most by making them visible components, determining causes and results, and then assigning priorities only to the causes, not to the results.

A simple way to assign priorities is to use the categories of "Seriousness," "Urgency," and "Growth." Rate each suspected cause with reference to these three categories in terms of high, medium, or low. To do this, ask the following types of questions concerning each cause:

Seriousness: How serious is this cause in respect to the other causes?
How big is it?
How bad is it?
How frequently is it occurring?
Dollarwise, how important is this piece of the problem?

Urgency: Do I have to drop everything else and take care of this today?
Can I do it just as well next week?
Can this part of the problem wait until next month?

Growth: If I don't take care of it now, will it get worse?
Will it soon spread out of control?

Rick finds that he can now analyze his problem fairly easily by using the "Seriousness / Urgency / Growth" (S.U.G.) system to rate each cause H (high), M (medium), or L (low). It seems to work best to rate the "Seriousness" of each cause first, next rate "Urgency," and last rate "Growth."

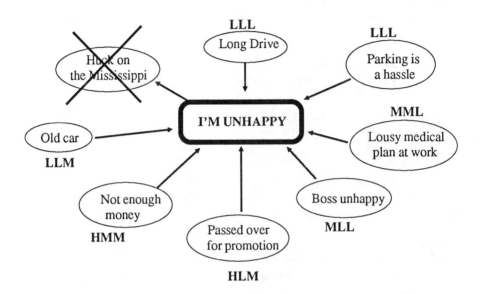

At this point, note that Rick rated two parts of his problem as "high" in seriousness: "Not enough money," and "Passed over for promotion." But his urgency rating was M for "Not enough money," and L in "Passed over for promotion." You may feel that if the seriousness of a problem is high, then the urgency must be high, and the growth factor must also be high. Be careful not to allow a high seriousness rating to influence your ratings of urgency and growth. In Rick's case, "Not enough money" was serious to him. But he felt that the urgency of this cause was only M, and that the growth factor was also only M.

Similarly, even though he rated "Passed over for promotion" as high in seriousness, he rated it low in urgency. Rick needs to do something about this piece of the problem. But realistically, it is not something that must be taken care of today—or even this week. In fact, it might be better if he would give this cause some time and solid thought before doing anything about it. Rick wisely rated this piece of the problem as low in growth. Yes, the problem is bad; but, no, the problem is not likely to get any worse. It is probably as bad as it is ever going to be right now. Therefore, it has low growth potential.

Step 5.   Decide which of the causes are: Problems; Decisions; Plans; New Messes

The final step in Situation Analysis is to label each of the major causes of the situation as follows:

Problems to be diagnosed. For example, "Passed over for promotion" may be a very real problem because Rick doesn't really know what the cause is. He thinks it is an EEO numbers situation; but that is only an assumption at this point. He needs to learn why he was passed over for promotion. Only when he determines why this occurred is he ready to take some kind of action to address this problem.

Decisions that must be made. For example, Rick's new medical plan will require his family to make some decisions about their future coverage.

Plans to be implemented. For example, Rick knows why the car requires a lot of maintenance (100,000 miles). And he knows what he wants to do about it (buy a new car). But buying a new car will require careful planning in order to make it happen.

New Messes (new situations that must be further broken down). For example, "Not enough money" may be a new situation to be analyzed, with its own set of causes and results.

Following is Rick's labeling of his problem causes as either problems, decisions, plans, or new messes.

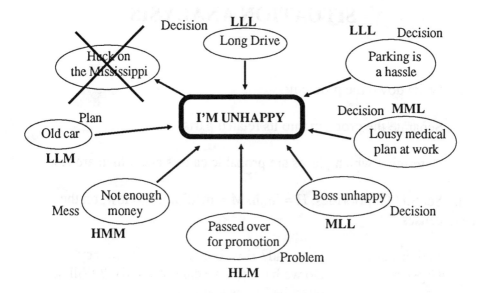

After you have analyzed the parts of your problem using Situation Analysis, you are ready to spend your time on the high priority causes. S.A. will not hand you some predetermined solution to your problem. But it does help you make the various parts of your problem visible, evaluate each part in a meaningful way, and decide where to focus your energy.

Each priority part of the Situation Analysis can then be looked at as an opportunity—an opportunity to do something differently and better.

The following page is a work sheet that you can duplicate for use in analyzing your problem situations.

SITUATION ANALYSIS

1. Write down the problem.

2. Separate the problem into its related parts.

3. Determine which pieces are probable causes and which are results.

4. Set S.U.G. priorities, H = high, M = medium, L = low, on the causes.

   Seriousness   — How bad? How big? How much money?
   Urgency   — Do we have to take care of it today? Will next week be just as good a time?
   Growth   — Is it getting worse? Or is it as bad as it is going to get?

5. Label the major causes: "Problem"; "Decision"; "Plan"; new "Mess."

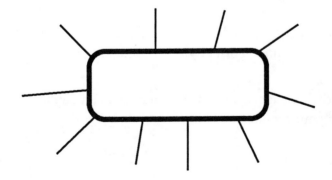

FINDING CAUSES

When trying to remedy a problem, many people jump into action without thinking. They just can't seem to help it: they want to be "doing" something—anything. In fact, taking action without thinking, no matter how unproductive, can become a way of life. Before—repeat, *before*—you take action to solve a problem, look for causes. When you find the causes, fix the cause that is most clearly connected to the problem.

When you problem solve, you are finding the cause of a problem—not analyzing a situation, making a decision, or implementing a plan. You are problem solving when:

1. *You have a deviation from the standard.*

   Something should be happening, but it isn't. It was supposed to have happened, but it didn't. It wasn't supposed to happen, but it did. All of these are deviations from standard.

2. *You find that the cause is uncertain.*

   If you already know the cause, then your next step is to make a decision by selecting the best way to fix the problem.

3. *You are concerned.*

   If you see a deviation from standard, and you don't know for sure why it happened, but you are not concerned about it—you have no problem.

You can find the cause of a problem by following these seven steps:

1. *Make a written problem statement.*

   In writing out your problem statement, make it specific and negative. Write "Passed over for promotion to supervisor," not just "Lost promotion." This not only helps pinpoint the problem, but also highlights what the real issue is.

2. *Ask what, where, and when the problem is occurring: and what, where, and when the problem is not occurring.*

   At times causes can be located more quickly if you clarify what is not the problem as well as what is. The better you define the boundaries of a problem by specifying what the problem is not, the better you can determine the most probable causes.

   Also in Step 2 you ask, "What is the extent of the problem?" In other words, how bad or serious is the problem? This information can keep you from developing a $500 solution to fix a $3 problem.

   These What? / Where?/ When?/ Extent? questions help you locate and isolate the problem area, and thus show you where to look for causes. An electronics technician calls it "troubleshooting"; a doctor calls it "diagnosing." You might say it is "working smarter, not harder."

   For example, suppose you have a bad pain. Now, what kind of questions would your doctor ask before he says, "Take two aspirins and call me in the morning."

   Your doctor might ask, "Where does it hurt? When does it bother you? When did you first notice it? How much does it hurt?" But good doctors don't stop there. They also ask questions about what the problem is *not*. For example, your doctor would probably ask, "Does it hurt anywhere else?" and "Have you ever had this pain before?"

From asking questions, your doctor might discover that your problem is in your right elbow, and not any other part of your body. It hurts all day; not only certain times of the day. The pain first started six weeks ago, and you never had it before—except when you were in high school.

3. *Examine closely the* **differences** *between where the problem is and where it is not.*

   If a problem exists in one area and not in another, the difference between the two areas can produce clues to help locate the cause. So you ask: "What peculiar differences exist between where the problem is occurring, and where it is not occurring?" Or, "What is different about when the problem occurs and when it doesn't?"

   In the doctor example from Step 2, by specifying what, where, when, and to what extent the problem is and is not, your doctor is then able to determine the particular differences. For example, the doctor might discover that you are right handed, and you were a softball pitcher in high school. Then, by determining the peculiar differences between what the problem is and is not, your doctor is then able to look for changes in and around the differences.

4. *Look carefully for* **changes** *that have occurred in and around the environment of the problem.*

   Changes can cause problems. In fact, problems—by definition—are always caused by changes. Remember that problems where no change has occurred are not true problems. They are decisions that must be made or plans that should be implemented. For example, guess what your doctor discovered you were doing with your kid every night after supper for the past six weeks? Right! You have Little League elbow.

5. *Develop "probable cause statements" concerning the changes discovered in Step 4 by linking each change to the problem.*

Every change will produce its own unique probable cause statement.

In the doctor example, a probable cause statement would be:

"Pitching softball with your child each night after supper has resulted in tendinitis in your elbow."

6. *Test each probable cause statement against all of the* is *and* is not *facts, in order to determine the most probable cause.*

For example, your doctor could say:

"If it is tendinitis, would that account for the fact that the pain is in the right elbow and not the left?" Yes. "That it hurts constantly and not only certain times in the day?" Yes. "That the pain first started six weeks ago and you had never had it before except when you were a pitcher in high school?" Yes.

Since tendinitis checks out against the known set of facts, the doctor would then move to the next step—verifying that it really is the cause.

7. *Verify the most probable cause to make sure it is the real cause.*

Your doctor could verify the cause by gently probing your elbow, or even by taking X rays.

Note that these seven steps are usually inexpensive: they just require mental effort—pencil and paper, and possibly phone calls to gather information. Of course, taking action to remedy the problem may involve financial commitment. And many lost dollars if you fail to carefully go through the problem solving process!

Yet many people start their problem solving efforts by throwing money into an ill-conceived solution before thinking through the problem. They jump in with both feet to take action. Any action! And they often end up spending much more time and money than is necessary—and the problem still isn't solved.

In brief outline, the above seven-step process looks like this:

1. PROBLEM STATEMENT: _____

2.	IS	IS NOT	3. DIFFERENCE	4. CHANGES
What?	_____	_____	_____	_____
— Defect	_____	_____	_____	_____
— Object	_____	_____	_____	_____
Where?	_____	_____	_____	_____
When?	_____	_____	_____	_____
Extent?	_____	_____	_____	_____

5. Probable Causes
1. _____
2. _____
3. _____

6. Test the probable cause statements against the initial set of facts.

7. Verify the most probable cause.

Now let's illustrate the seven-step problem solving technique by taking a hypothetical example.

THE CASE OF THE SODDEN SHEETS

It has been a long hot day at the office, and I breathe a sigh of relief as I finish writing up the last paragraph of an eight-page report my boss asked for yesterday. Because of an unusual warm spell at the end of a Minnesota winter, the office has been hot and sticky all day. No time for relaxing tonight, either, because the PTA meeting starts at 8:30. Before that, I have to drive over to the Men's Store and pick up my new suit so I will have it for a special meeting tomorrow. And sometime during the running around I want to eat supper with the family. Fortunately, at least, no evening trip to the doctor tonight—the kids have been a lot better since I installed a new humidifier on the basement furnace two months ago.

The phone rings, I answer, it's my wife. She is really upset! She tells me there's a leak in the upstairs bedroom ceiling making a wet spot in the plaster that's getting bigger and bigger. She put a pan on the floor under the leak and wants to know how soon I can be home. I tell her I'm on my way.

As I leave the parking lot, I am thinking hard about the leak— and the time-bind I'm in. A number of solutions pop into my mind. I could shovel the snow off the roof. Or call a plumber; or a roofer. Or just empty out the bucket every day. Or maybe do nothing, and let the bed get wet! One thing is certain, at least: the V.P. is going to run the school PTA meeting tonight!

The bedroom ceiling's surface is textured plaster, I think to myself. If the drip continues, there will be a hole in the ceiling. And I can't fix a hole in textured plaster (rough finished with a swirled pattern). I'll have to replace the entire ceiling.

What should I do about the leak?

Well, I think, I can't jump to conclusions or do anything until the *cause* of the problem is determined. "Calling a plumber" implies I know there is a leak in the water system. "Shoveling snow off the roof" or "calling a roofer" suggests that there's a hole in the roof. But since the cause of the problem is not known, the first thing to do is to determine the most probable cause.

Because the attic floor was not made to be walked on (we couldn't store boxes up there), I have never been up there. The attic access door is in the ceiling of the hall closet; and using a step ladder, I crawl up into the attic, flashlight in hand. Directing the light to the roof area above the bedroom, what do I see? Nothing! That's right, nothing. The attic ceiling is perfectly dry.

"That's strange," I say to myself. "There's water down there in the bedroom—and it's dry up here!" I then direct the light to the outside attic wall, and see a remarkable sight. Ice! Thick ice covering the wall. "Look at that ice!" I think to myself. "And if there's ice on that wall, there must be ice on the wall at the other end of the attic, too." I let the flashlight shine toward the other end—and guess what? Right: *no* ice. I think, "Now this is really strange. There's ice on one wall, but no ice on the other."

I think to myself, "If there's ice on the west wall, and no ice on the east, there's obviously a reason. There must be some difference between the west end of the attic and the east end." Then I notice that the west end of the attic end seems less dark than the east end. Looking more closely, I suddenly become aware that there is no insulation over the place where the bedroom light fixture was—and I can see light shining through from the bedroom.

"OK," I think, "The heat from the bedroom could account for moist air condensing and freezing on the west wall, while not on the east. But why this year and not previous years? What has changed, causing this difference in the two walls?"

Now let's make this problem "visible" by describing it in writing:

	THE PROBLEM IS:	THE PROBLEM IS NOT:	DIFFERENCE:	CHANGE:
WHAT:	Water	Dryness		
WHERE:	Bedroom	Any other room		
	Bedroom ceiling	Attic ceiling		
	Ice on west wall	Ice on east wall	Insulation	None
WHEN:	This year	Previous years		
EXTENT:	Very serious (to replace entire ceiling: over $1,000)	OK		

What do *you* think has changed? What one thing changed that caused this "Case of the Sodden Sheets?" Yes—the new humidifier! And this is what our problem specification now looks like:

	THE PROBLEM IS:	THE PROBLEM IS NOT:	DIFFERENCE:	CHANGE:
WHAT:	Water	Dryness		
WHERE:	Bedroom	Any other room		
	Bedroom ceiling	Attic ceiling		
	Ice on west wall	Ice on east wall	Insulation	None
WHEN:	This year	Previous years	MOISTURE	NEW HUMIDIFIER
EXTENT:	Very serious (to replace entire ceiling: over $1,000)	OK		

We are now ready for Step 5: Write out a "probable cause statement." After the above analysis, here is what a probable cause statement will look like:

CHANGE ⟶ **COMMON SENSE LINK** ⟶ **END RESULT**

CHANGE	COMMON SENSE LINK	END RESULT
New humidifier installed last year increased moisture content in the air.	The warm, moist air rose through the uninsulated light fixture in the master bedroom.	The air froze with the winter weather, and is now thawing during the current warm spell.

In Step 6, we will mentally test the probable cause statement against all the "is" and "is not" facts to determine if it fits the problem's specification. We say, "If the new humidifier is causing the problem, does that explain..."

Water rather than dryness? Yes!
In the bedroom and not any other room? Yes!
On the bedroom ceiling, and not the attic ceiling? Yes!
Ice on the attic's west wall and not the east one? Yes!
This year, and not previous years? Yes!

Since the answer is "Yes" to each set of "is" and "is not" facts, it appears that this probable cause tests positive against the known problem description.

But we are still not ready to say that the new humidifier is the only cause—Not yet! For there is one more—very important—step in our problem analysis process: verification! We need to verify the most probable cause by asking additional questions, and obtaining additional information to see if it is the *real* cause.

Verification in our example might be as simple as calling a couple of humidifier distributors in Saint Paul and asking them if they have ever encountered this problem before. Or I could look up several humidifier installers in the phone book, and ask them if they have ever encountered an icing problem related to a humidifier.

When we feel reasonably certain that our most probable cause is *the* cause, then—and only then—are we ready to take action. In this case, the short-term action was to remove the remaining ice from the attic wall. The long-term solution was to place insulation above the light fixture.

As you can see from our example, there is a direct relationship between the cause of a problem and the observed effects. The effects point to a very particular kind of problem, and that special problem would produce only those effects.

As you've seen, the cause of any problem leaves an imprint of effects that can be viewed in four dimensions. The first dimension is *identity*. In "The Case of the Sodden Sheets," the problem's identity was a wet spot in the ceiling. The second dimension is *location*. The problem occurred in the bedroom ceiling, not in the attic ceiling—or in any other room. There is also a dimension of *timing*. The problem occurred this year, not in previous years.

And last, there is the *extent* of the problem—that is, its size and severity. In the case above, with a rough textured ceiling I could not simply patch the old plaster. That would have led to having to replace the entire ceiling, which would require major expenditures! So this problem was serious. But because it was analyzed carefully, and verified by using the above problem solving process, the action taken cost only the price of a little insulation (pennies)—rather than $1,000-plus, and no effective solution to the problem!

One more point. Problems that fit the criteria of a problem (deviation from the standard, unknown cause, you are concerned about it) don't stay problems for long. You normally find the causes, and fix them. But when you identify a list of existing problems, you will often find that your list includes a number of old problems. These old problems usually have known causes, but haven't been solved simply because you are unable to make decisions about them. These problems are not true problems at all. They require decisions (which will be covered in the next chapter), not problem solving.

In this chapter you have seen the:

- importance of thinking through a problem before attempting to solve it.
- need to make the problem visible in writing.
- great value of using a problem solving process.
- importance of not jumping to conclusions and taking premature, costly action.

A problem solving process allows you to isolate the problem by describing what, where, when, and to what extent the problem *is* and *is not*. You then know that the problem lies within this boundary. You need only ask the right questions—What? Where? When? and to what Extent?

Here's an outline of the process:

1. PROBLEM STATEMENT
   "What is wrong?"

2. DESCRIPTION

WHAT DEFECT?	"What symptoms do we have?"
	"What symptoms don't we have that we might expect?"
WHAT OBJECT?	"What/who has failed?"
	"What/who has not failed?"
WHERE?	"Where do we have the problem?"
	"Where don't we have the problem?"
WHEN?	"When did it start?"
	"When was everything OK?"
EXTENT?	"How serious is it?"
	"How big is it?"
	"What is normal?"

3. DIFFERENCES?   "What is strange/different/unusual/peculiar about this problem?"
   "Why is it doing this, and not that?
   "Why did this fail, and not that?"

	"Why did it happen here, and not there?"
	"Why did it start then, and not before?"
	"Why is it this much bigger or more serious than normal?"
4. CHANGES?	"What has changed?"
	"How has it changed?"
	"When did it change?"
5. PROBABLE CAUSES?	"How could this change cause the problem?"
6. MENTALLY TESTING	"If this is the cause, does it explain all the facts of our problem-description?"
7. VERIFICATION	"Who else can we talk to, what records can we check, what evidence can we find to determine that this is the real cause of our problem?"

Try using the seven-step problem solving grid on the following page to solve some problem you have. You may find blanks in the grid. Since many people are task-oriented and want to solve the problem immediately, these can cause frustration. This is not only a normal reaction; it is often a positive one, since it gives you clear direction on where to go and whom to ask for the missing information. In other words, the grid process protects you from jumping to conclusions and taking the right action on the wrong cause!

By using this seven-step diagnostic process, you can resolve problems quicker; correct causes, not just effects; solve problems so they stay solved; and not create new problems by taking the wrong action.

A problem exists when: (1) a deviation from an expected standard has occurred; (2) the cause of that deviation is uncertain; and (3) the deviation concerns you.

1. PROBLEM STATEMENT

	2.		3. DIFFERENCES	4. CHANGES	STEPS IN DIAGNOSING CAUSE
	IS	IS NOT			1. Write a specific negative problem statement.
W H A T ? ? DEFECT (Symptoms)					2. Describe the problem by writing what, where, when and to what extent the problem IS and IS NOT.
OBJECT (Who/What?)					3. Determine any peculiar and pertinent differences between what the problem IS and what the problem IS NOT.
WHERE?					4. Look carefully for changes that have occurred in and around the differences.
WHEN?					5. Write a probable cause statement for each change discovered in step 4 above.
EXTENT? (Seriousness)					6. Test each probable cause statement against each specific set of IS and IS NOT facts, and determine the most probable cause.
					7. Verify the most probable cause statement, take appropriate action, and monitor results.

5. PROBABLE CAUSE STATEMENTS (one for each change)

6. Test each probable cause statement against each set of "IS" and "IS NOT" facts.

CHANGE	LINK	END RESULT

7. Most probable cause statements:
— What can be done to verify that this is the cause?
— Given this is the cause, what action(s) can be taken to correct the original problem?

CHAPTER 7
MAKING GOOD DECISIONS

THE FOUR-STEP DECISION PROCESS

Charles Kepner and Benjamin Tregoe have greatly influenced the field of modern decision making. They have formulated their ideas into a four-stage process—called the "Kepner-Tregoe (KT) Decision Analysis." These four steps are:

1. Write a decision statement.
2. Develop objectives.
3. Create alternatives.
4. Examine risks.

Let's look at the Kepner-Tregoe process, presented in their book, *The New Rational Manager,* beginning with some important ideas on how to write a decision statement.

1. Writing a Decision Statement

As with problem solving, the first step is to make the decision statement visible—write it down. So let's begin by examining how to write this statement.

One mistake that is easy to make when writing decision statements is to write what are called "binary statements." "Binary" is a word used to describe something that is made up of two parts. Binary statements are decisions like: "Accept or reject that proposal"; "Go to San Francisco or not"; "Vote 'yes' or 'no' on gun control"; or, "Quit job or not." These statements, by the way they are worded, tend to force your thinking into a premature comparison of only two alternatives.

To make more effective decisions, keep your statements open for more than two alternatives. For example, you could take the binary decision statement, "Accept or reject that proposal," and rewrite it so as to give you other alternatives. If you start decision statements with the words, "Select the best..." you are almost guaranteed to have an "open" decision statement. Thus, the first binary statement above can be written, "Select the best proposal." And the second binary decision statement, "Go to San Francisco or not," becomes "Select the best city to visit." Now you are free to choose: to go to San Francisco, New York, New Orleans—or stay home.

How would you turn "Vote 'yes' or 'no' on gun control" into an open decision statement? Sometimes it helps to ask yourself a question like, "Why would someone want gun control?" (We're not taking a stand here.) Now note that gun control is one possible solution to at least two different problems—reducing crime, and preventing gun accidents. But as Dr. Peter Drucker said, "Trying to solve two problems with one solution very seldom works."

Rather than limiting your decision statement to only one solution, it is better to find the main problems being faced, and to put each problem's solution in its own decision statement. This allows you to develop a list of alternative solutions for each decision statement.

PROBLEMS:	High crime rate	Gun accidents
DECISION STATEMENTS:	Select best way to reduce crime.	Select best way to reduce gun accidents.
ALTERNATIVES:	1. Gun control 2. Stiffer penalties 3. More police 4. Better security	1. Gun control 2. Education 3. "Safety" ammunition 4. Child-proof guns

Notice the many different alternatives made available by making decision statements "open." You could still implement gun control if you wish. But by transforming your initial gun control statement into two pertinent open statements, you open up a variety of courses of action.

2. Developing Objectives

Step 2 in decision making is to decide what you want to accomplish by your decision—your goals, objectives, desired results—before creating alternative solutions. Developing objectives before alternatives counteracts the tendency to choose only those objectives which fit your pre-selected solutions.

Get help from others in writing out your list of objectives. And include all important items that are considerations in making the decision. The more sound data you have here, the better your final decision will be.

Objectives come from questions like these:

"What factors should I consider?"
    Examples:
      — Time   — Location
      — Approvals

"What results are desired?"
    Examples:
      — Efficiency   — Saving money
      — Safety   — Satisfaction
      — Recognition — High morale

"What resources are available?"   "What restrictions are there?"
   Examples: Examples:

— People	— Budget	— Law	— Policy
— Equipment	— Materials	— Standards	— Values
— Skills	— Knowledge	— Ethics	

Before going on to the last two steps, let's look at an example of decision making. Read the following case study, noting what you feel are the important objectives in this situation.

THE CASE OF THE DIFFICULT DWELLING DECISION

Matt and his wife Cathleen sat at the kitchen table talking about their decision to buy a home. Their lease would expire in four months, the house had been sold, and the new owners were eager to move in.

Matt knew that Cathleen was looking forward to leaving their cramped three-bedroom ranch home. With four children—two girls, ages 5 and 16, and two boys, 9 and 15—it had really been tough on her. It also had been hard on the teenage children, who had to share their rooms with their younger siblings. But the boys were a particular problem for Cathleen. They fought constantly, each blaming the other for messing up the room, and neither accepting responsibility for straightening it up. Fortunately, they had a large yard for the dogs!

Matt hoped that they could locate a house they could afford on at least a half-acre lot. If they could find a 90% mortgage, they could manage it. It would use up all their savings; and with no way of borrowing extra money for emergencies, it would be risky. But it would be well worth it.

Matt also hoped they could get a garage that would hold the boat, since he hated leaving it out in the rain. And Cathleen wanted at least two baths. In fact, she said that if a house didn't have two full baths, she wouldn't even consider it. She was sick of "Grand Central Station," as she called their single bathroom. And wherever the house was, it must have public sewage, water, and gas. Matt had sworn never to have a septic system again. And all their appliances used gas.

It would also be nice to be located within a couple of miles of a shopping area. One redeeming factor about their present home was its location only two blocks from a small shopping center.

Fortunately, since the school system in the area was excellent, schools were not a problem.

To get the size home they wanted for the money they had to spend, Matt knew they would have to buy a considerable distance from town. He didn't mind the drive—so long as the house wasn't more than 45 minutes from work by the expressway, and he didn't have to drive with the sun in his eyes in the morning and evening.

Thus, Matt and Cathleen's objectives in buying a home are the following:

1. Available in 4 months
2. Minimum of 4 bedrooms
3. Large yard
4. 90% mortgage available
5. Garage for the boat
6. Two baths
7. Public utilities (sewage, water, gas)
8. Near a shopping area
9. Not more that 45 minutes from work
10. Not west of town

When a list of objectives has been established, the next step is to determine which of them is *required,* and which are simply *desired.* Then when you later develop alternative solutions, each solution must meet the required objectives, or it is not acceptable. This will save lots of time and energy by limiting your thought and discussion only to those alternatives that actually meet your required objectives.

"Must" objectives are established by basic needs, budget, time, policy, rules, law. "Want" objectives are often comparisons, such as low cost, least time, largest, nice, best, etc.

Because "must" objectives limit alternatives, it is wise to restrict their number when possible. Musts also need to be specific and measurable (e.g., "Available in 4 months," not "Available soon").

Looking at the list above, which items do you think were Matt and Cathleen's *must* objectives, and which were their *want* objectives?

If you were making this judgment for yourself, of course, your *must* and *want* objectives would probably be different from Matt and Cathleen's. In their case, however, they felt that "Available in 4 months," "Minimum of 4 bedrooms," "90% mortgage available," and "Two baths" were their *musts*.

3. Creating Alternatives

In this step you create alternatives to fulfill your objectives. At this point, it is often helpful to think in terms of the following classifications:

- **corrective** alternatives that solve the problem;
- **interim** alternatives that don't remedy the problem, but do buy time; and
- **adaptive** alternatives which allow us to live with the problem.

For example, if the problem is a fire, I can take corrective action by putting the fire out with water. Or I could take interim action, by doing something to restrict air flow to the fire. Or I could take adaptive action by deciding to let the building burn down—and roast hot dogs. By being aware of all three of these classes of alternatives, we can significantly increase the number of available approaches.

In developing creative alternatives, two things are helpful. First, "brainstorm" a list of possibilities, and later evaluate and combine them to create workable solutions. Second, get help! Talk to people whose opinions and judgment you trust. Since you have made your decision process visible (in writing) from the beginning, you can show others both the problem and the alternatives you are considering, and ask them for additional ideas.

It is much easier to make good decisions after you have clarified your objectives and created alternatives. For example, consider "The Case of the Difficult Dwelling Decision" just presented. Evaluate the following three alternatives, given Matt and Cathleen's list of objectives. Should any of these homes be eliminated because it fails to satisfy at least one of their *must* objectives?

1. An attractive new tri-level, with a big yard, 4 bedrooms (and a possible 5th bedroom in the attic), and 2 1/2 baths. 90% mortgage. No garage. Gas and sewage available. Approximately 15 miles from work. No shopping area nearby. Possession immediate. Located in an established, older neighborhood.

2. A new house that Matt really likes, with 4 bedrooms and a large 2-car garage. In addition, it has 2 baths, a shopping mall 4 blocks away, 90% mortgage available, a small yard, and gas and sewage. It is only 30 minutes from work, and will be available in three months. Unfortunately, its location will mean that Matt will have to drive to and from work with the sun in his eyes.

3. The third house is Cathleen's choice, even though it is not new. It is about 6 years old, with 5 bedrooms and two baths, and is in a beautiful neighborhood. The extremely large yard has many trees (with a swing for the children, and a tree house), and a chain-link fence for the dogs. Matt also likes the fully developed yard, with a single car garage plus tool shed in back; and the fact that it was only 6 miles from work. A 90% mortgage can be obtained, and the owner has agreed to pay most of the closing costs. A shopping center and the elementary school are only three blocks away. Gas and public sewage are available. The present owner has kept the house

spotless. But they are building a new home and hope to move out within 4 months. For the money they are asking, the house is a bargain.

Must any of these 3 homes be eliminated from consideration because it fails to meet Matt and Cathleen's *must* objectives?

Matt and Cathleen are faced with a difficult decision. Emotionally, they want house #3. But they really cannot consider this alternative, because it doesn't meet one of their *must* objectives—"Available in 4 months." Earlier we said that it is not desirable to have *must* objectives that are not absolutely necessary, because they eliminate alternatives. So unless Matt and Cathleen can find a way out of their dilemma by making the 4 months a *want* objective, they cannot select this alternative—and must confine their attention to houses #1 and #2, both of which meet all of their *must* objectives.

This decision is typical of the ones you face at work as well as at home. Emotionally, you want to select a particular alternative—and too often do, even when the absence of *must* qualities suggests it will not work out well. Decisions turn out better when you first take the time to determine objectives, prioritize them, create a number of alternatives, and then rationally evaluate each one in terms of *musts*. This process produces good decisions because it helps you to figure out what is really important.

4. Analyzing Risk

The fourth and last step in the decision process is to consider carefully the risk involved with each of the leading alternatives. This is the most neglected step in decision making—because we tend to look at life's new possibilities and beginnings in glowing terms. Thus, you must examine the risks in your decisions before implementing them. To do this, simply ask, "What can go wrong?" And here again, seek out help from others with experience, since several individuals can often foresee future problems better than one person working alone.

When first considering potential risks, deal with one alternative at a time. That is, do not attempt initially to look at the possibility of each risk occurring in every alternative. Then when you have completed your list of potential risks (problems) for the first alternative, evaluate each potential problem in terms of the probability of it happening, and its seriousness if it does happen. Then repeat the same process with each of your other leading alternatives.

In "The Case of the Difficult Dwelling Decision," Matt and Cathleen were left with two alternatives—homes #1 and #2. Their last step, then, was to evaluate the risks in selecting each of these alternatives by asking: "If we buy this particular house, what could go wrong?" After talking with friends and some professionals, they developed the following "risk list." (Note that even though we show the following risks together in one chart, each alternative's risks should be analyzed separately.)

Alternative #1: Risks	Probability (of its happening)	Seriousness (if it happens)
1. Builder has a poor reputation; this house may turn out to be a lemon.	LOW	HIGH
2. Tri-level houses are difficult to heat.	HIGH	LOW
3. Since this is a new house in an established neighborhood, we might get complaints about our dogs. (We didn't see any other dogs when we drove around.)	MEDIUM	MEDIUM
4. When we looked at the house on Saturday, we didn't notice many children either. How will the neighbors feel about four active children?	LOW	MEDIUM

Alternative #2: Risks		
1. Expensive fire insurance since the fire department is far from the house.	HIGH	LOW

Though we can't make Matt and Cathleen's decision for them, their own evaluation of risks suggests that alternative #2 may be the best house for their needs because of the greater number of potential problems with alternative #1.

This four-step process—writing an "open" decision statement, developing objectives, creating and evaluating alternatives, and analyzing risk—is usually the best way to make a well-balanced decision.

But there are, of course, always exceptions. Therefore, we will conclude this chapter by looking briefly at another decision-making technique, especially useful when the decision involves only two alternatives or deals with less logical factors than normal.

FORCE FIELD ANALYSIS

"Force field analysis" is, in fact, a simple and easy way to make good decisions. You only need to think of—and make visible—all of the reasons for choosing one alternative, and then all the reasons against doing so.

Let's look at a typical example. Suppose you are deciding whether or not to seek a promotion to supervisor. Your decision can be diagrammed as follows:

"Seek a promotion to supervisor."

Reasons for:	Reasons against:
More money	
	Hassles with employees
Prestige	
	No longer working with friends
More authority	
	More paperwork
Recognition	
	Longer working hours
Challenge	
	More politics on the job
	Being a supervisor is scary
	Not as much time for family

Note that the length of the arrow indicates the relative importance of this factor to you. Analyze each factor for:

1) **Realism** (Is it a fact? Your opinion? A rumor?)
2) **Control** (Can you do anything about this factor? Make a

positive element even more positive? Or a negative factor
less negative?)

As in the Four-Step Decision Making process, seek help! Talk to
people who have faced similar decisions in the past. Ask them about
additional factors to consider; and get their insight into evaluating the
relative strength of each of your factors.

The following two pages are work sheets for utilizing, first, the
Four-Step Decision Making process, and then the Force Field
Analysis. Try using them to make a decision you currently face.

THE FOUR-STEP DECISION PROCESS

Decision Statement: _____
_____
_____

	Must have	Want to have

Objectives: _____ ___ ___
_____ ___ ___
_____ ___ ___
_____ ___ ___
_____ ___ ___
_____ ___ ___
_____ ___ ___
_____ ___ ___
_____ ___ ___

Alternatives: 1. _____
_____

2. _____
_____

3. _____
_____

4 _____
_____

Risks with leading alternatives: (Rate each risk in terms of the Probability of its happening, and its Seriousness if it does happen, using H = High, M = Medium, and L = Low.)

Alternative #	P S (H,M,L)	Alternative #	P S (H,M,L)
_____	_ | _	_____	_ | _
_____	_ | _	_____	_ | _
_____	_ | _	_____	_ | _
_____	_ | _	_____	_ | _
_____	_ | _	_____	_ | _

FORCE FIELD ANALYSIS

Draw horizontal arrows on each side of the vertical line corresponding to the reasons for (left side), and the reasons against (right side) your decision.

Use the arrow's length to indicate the relative importance of each reason.

Seek help; talk with others.

Decision Statement: _____

_____

_____

Reasons For:	Reasons Against:

Analyze each factor for realism. Is it a fact? Your opinion? A rumor? How could you verify those factors that are opinions or rumors?

_____

_____

_____

What factors can you control? i.e., how can you make a positive factor even more positive? Or a negative factor less negative?

_____

_____

_____

CHAPTER 8
THE IMPORTANCE OF
PLANNING

Good planning is based on a four-stage process:
- determining your goals and setting priorities
- writing your priority goals in an objective form
- developing steps to reach your objectives
- anticipating potential problems

In this chapter, we will review each of these stages of successful planning. Then you can use the work sheet at the end of the chapter to practice planning on your job—or with any life-goals.

In all human activity, planning is critical for several important reasons.

1. *Knowing where you are going helps you get there.* Alice said to the Cheshire cat in Lewis Carroll's *Through the Looking Glass*:

   > "Tell me, please, which way it is I ought to go from here."
   > "Where is it you want to go?" said the cat.
   > "I don't care much where," said Alice.
   > "Then it doesn't matter which way you go!" said the cat.

   The cat was telling Alice that it didn't make much difference what she did, since she didn't know where she wanted to go. But it makes a very great difference on the job to know where you want to go. If you are not moving toward a specific goal, then you have no way of knowing whether your work is productive or not. Successful people plan everything they do—every day. Plans make destinations clear. They suggest how to get there, and they allow you to measure the success of your efforts.

2. *Planning enables you to experience a daily sense of accomplishment.* Your plans will guide you in choosing the work today that will lead to your goals—thus providing a continuous feeling of

fulfillment. Distant, general aims alone don't have much personal influence on your immediate activities. But when you take a distant goal and specify its sub-goals, along with a step-by-step plan to reach each sub-goal, then you'll see that certain of these steps need to be worked on this week—or today. By successfully carrying out today's steps in your plan, you are immediately rewarded with a sense of accomplishment.

3. *Good planning prevents procrastination.* The most important things in life (like distant goals and objectives) do not create a sense of urgency until you begin to see how to reach them. Because they appear so far in the future, you may feel it is all right to put off action on them until tomorrow—especially since there are so many seemingly urgent things to do right now. So, given the choice between "urgent" matters and distant aims (no matter how important), most people normally go with the urgent and postpone the important. But when you bring your ultimate goals and objectives into the present by creating step-by-step plans, then you may realize that acting on a goal is urgent now.

4. *Planning prevents problems.* Well thought-out plans help you anticipate potential problems before they happen. Problems are much less likely to happen if you take the time to analyze them by thinking them through, talking with others, and developing creative solutions.

Most people agree that good planning is important to the success of any project. And yet, all too often we don't spend sufficient time in planning. Why not? There are a number of reasons:

- You may have to commit yourself to doing something today that you really don't want to do. And so, "No problem is so big that it can't be ignored"!

- You can seem like a "hero" by putting out fires caused through lack of planning. You can even make a career out of permitting crises which you then step into and dramatically end.

- It simply seems easier to operate by the seat of your pants and bounce along from one crisis to the next.

- It takes time to write goal statements, and then develop plans and strategies.

- Your performance on the job is often evaluated in terms of what you appear to be **doing**, rather than on how well you plan. For example, you are sitting at your desk planning how you are going to do a high-priority job, and your boss walks up and says, "Don't just sit there. Get busy and *do* something!"

- You may not know how to plan effectively.

So let's look at the steps in good planning.

Determining Your Goals and Setting Priorities

The first step in real planning is to find a quiet place, and brainstorm a list of the most important things you want to do and be. As you list your goals, don't stop to evaluate or judge them. Write down everything that occurs to you, even if it may seem silly. If you have a burning secret desire—write it down! Focus on all areas of your life, not just your job. Consider family, education, work, hobbies, personal growth—whatever goals are important to you.

Don't worry about writing measurable objective statements at this point. As long as you know what you mean by what you wrote, that's fine. And this is *your* list; don't show it to anybody.

For example, here is my list of personal goals:

* 1. Improve my relationship with my children
  2. Write another book
  3. Gross X amount of dollars next year
  4. Attend the next International Training Federation meeting
  5. Take a rubber-raft trip on a white water river
  6. Try out for a part in a local theater production
  7. Visit three foreign countries next year
  8. Buy a 1980 Corvette
  9. Learn how to fly
  10. Take a ride in a glider
  11. Be a good grandfather
  12. Visit my son in Australia
  13. Reduce my travel time to not more than one trip per quarter
  14. Build a cider press before next fall
  15. Build a small paddle wheel boat to use for recreation on the river
  *16. Learn Russian
  17. Play a solo guitar piece in the upcoming Christmas music festival
  *18. Give more quality time and effort to my marriage
  19. Lose 15 pounds

After you have spent a few minutes freely creating your personal goal list, select the top three items and mark them with an check (✔) or asterisk (as I have). You can use the form on the next page to create your list of what you most want to do and be.

MY PERSONAL AND JOB-RELATED GOALS

Don't stop to judge or evaluate your goals as you write them down. Just list those things you want to do, be, or become, as they occur to you. Consider all areas of your life: business; family; education; hobbies; religion; etc. for other possibilities.

1. _____
2. _____
3. _____
4. _____
5. _____
6. _____
7. _____
8. _____
9. _____
10. _____
11. _____
12. _____
13. _____
14. _____
15. _____
16. _____
17. _____
18. _____

Now put a check mark or asterisk beside your top three goals at this time in your life.

Writing Your Priority Goals in an Objective Form

Now that you have brainstormed a list of the things you would like to be and do, and identified the most important ones, you are ready to enter into an eight-step planning process. The first step is to write out your highest-priority goals in an objective form.

An objective (or goal—we will use these two words interchangeably) is simply a statement of exactly what you want to accomplish. Such a statement should have the following three characteristics:

1. An objective statement should be **specific**, not general. For example, the statement: "Improve my relationship with my children" does not communicate enough information. How am I going to try to improve my relationship with them? What areas am I going to work on? How will I know when I have improved my relationship with them? By when do I want to see such improvement? And, what does the word "relationship" mean? Since my objective statement doesn't give enough specific information about my goal, it will be hard to actually know when I am successful—or even whether I am unsuccessful. Thus, in my objective statement I need to:

   — Determine what **actions** I am going to take—what I will do— in order to improve my relationship with my children. I need to specify behaviors. For example, I could:

      Read one recommended book on child-rearing and one on the problems of adolescence by the first of December;

      Attend at least one school activity involving each child this term;

      Quietly, attentively, ask each of the children how everything is going—every day, when possible.

   — Identify **end results**. For example:

      By next school year, each of the children will be taking the initiative to invite me to particular school activities;

      Each child will be voluntarily coming to confide in me concerning his or her problems, hopes, etc.

2. A good objective statement should also be **measurable** or **quantifiable.** To "learn Russian," sounds fine. But I really won't know when I have satisfactorily achieved this goal, because I haven't indicated my standard—or measure—of achievement. If I rewrite it, stating, "Obtain a certificate of completion in speaking Russian from Lincoln University within two years," my goal is measurable in two ways. First, I have used a word that specifies *behavior* (speaking, rather than learn). And second, I have committed myself to a specific *time period.* With my goal statement thus re-expressed in measurable terms, I am able to determine when I have achieved it.

3. Third, an objective statement should be truly **achievable.** There is little point in setting yourself up for failure. A good goal statement will extend and improve you, not break you. For example, note that my objective is to learn how to speak, not write Russian. As a dyslexic, my spelling skills in English are marginal. For me to learn how to spell Russian words correctly would be nearly impossible! If I wrote a goal statement on writing Russian, I'd be setting myself up for failure.

    You can develop several different types of job objectives:

    *   First are regular or *routine* objectives that simply specify the things you normally do on your job.

    *   Second are *problem-solving* objectives that you write to solve a specific problem.

    *   Next are *innovative* objectives, written to facilitate new, or creative ideas.

    *   Finally come *personal* objectives, which you write about you.

Since most of your growth on the job is connected with the last three kinds of objectives, it will be beneficial both to you and your organization to concentrate more of your efforts in these three areas, rather than on routine objectives.

Before you start to spend time working on your job-related objectives, it would be best to sit down with your boss and inquire what he or she feels about your priorities. Ask which of the objectives you have written are "must do," "ought to do," and "nice to do." Since your performance will be appraised in the future on what you do, it only makes sense to complete job objectives that meet with your boss's approval.

Put your energies into only two or three objectives at any one time. Your chances of success are much better if you concentrate on a few important ones rather than all at once. (Other less important objectives can usually be addressed in the future.)

Make copies of the "Planning Work Sheet" at the end of this chapter. Use one work sheet for each of your key objectives. Write your objectives in specific and measurable terms so that you and others can know when you have reached them.

Developing Steps to Reach Your Objectives

After you have determined which objectives you want to implement, you can then develop the steps you will take to achieve these objectives. As you identify the steps in your plan, set completion dates for each step. (But do not assign a final number to your steps at this point. You may need to add more steps later.)

As an example, I know a person—let's call her "Elizabeth"—whose objective was to become a supervisor in her organization within two years. The initial steps of her plan looked something like this:

1. OBJECTIVE

   To become a supervisor in my organization within two years.

2. STEPS OF PLAN (with completion dates)

Meet with boss to discuss my goal.	Sept. 15
Write 3 key objectives in my present job, and discuss with boss.	Sept. 30

Analyze my leadership skills; determine my
strengths and where I need improvement.   Oct. 15

Sign up for at least one supervisory workshop
(each year) at the university's management
center.   Dec. 1

Attend night classes and get the 24 credits I
need to finish my 2-year college degree,
starting this semester.   Jan. 15

Determine which supervisory positions might
open up within two years.   Mar. 1

Anticipating Potential Problems in Your Plans

Now you need to look carefully at the steps in your plan, noting any that could cause difficulties—let's call them "critical" steps. From past experience, sometimes you **know** that a particular step means trouble! (Maybe you took that step before and it led to a disaster.) If a step is completely new to you, look out. "Murphy's Law" may get you! Major steps, with lots of parts and pieces, are especially subject to the rule that "What can go wrong, will go wrong," particularly so if you have no experience with the step. You have also probably noted that problems can result when people have to communicate over distances by phone or letter; and also when there are a number of people involved.

If a step means operating close to the limits of your space, time, or money, you probably have trouble brewing. For example, if your plan requires that you order a new item that is exactly 3 feet wide, and your door is 3' and 1/2", you had better get an ax! Or if someone tells you the item you ordered will be here on Wednesday, and you have to have it Thursday, you might be wise to assume that it won't arrive until Friday. If a step in your plan "will only cost $99.95," and you have exactly $100.00, then you pretty well know what's going to happen!

All this potential problem analysis may sound negative. But the good news is that if you can anticipate potential problems before you implement your plan, you can often develop solutions that will increase the chances that you will achieve your goal.

In the example of Elizabeth, she selected as a critical step in her plan, "Attend night classes and get the 24 credits I need to finish my 2-year college degree." She viewed this step as a problem because it was new for her (she had never attended college at night). It was also a very important one. She worked for a boss who had once said in her presence, "Your chances of being selected a supervisor in this organization are a lot better if you have had some college."

Next, focus on the steps that may cause problems (critical steps), and list the potential problems. In Elizabeth's case, she wrote down the following problems:

3. CRITICAL STEP

"Attend night classes and get the 24 credits I need to finish my 2-year college degree, starting this semester."

4. POTENTIAL PROBLEMS
   A. Night school will be very hard on my family.
   B. I'll get bored and stop attending.
   C. It may take longer than 2 years to get the 24 credits I need.

The next step is to evaluate the probability and seriousness of each potential problem. That is, figure out what the probability is that the problem will occur, and how seriously it will effect the success of your plan if it does occur. To rate probability and seriousness, use H for high, M for medium, and L for low.

In the example of Elizabeth, she felt that night school would be a hardship for her family—not only in terms of cost, but also time.

Attending classes would take much time away from home, and the courses would also require a great deal of time for homework.

She felt that the chances of her getting bored with school, and therefore dropping out, were very low. But of course, if this did happen, it would have a serious impact on her plan, because her boss would see her as a failure in an area he considered very important. She thought she could finish the degree program within the two-year time limit; and if she didn't, she would be so close to finishing that her boss would still support her efforts. Her analysis now looked like this:

4. POTENTIAL PROBLEMS	5. EVALUATE EACH POTENTIAL PROBLEM AS TO THEIR PROBABILITY AND SERIOUSNESS (High, Medium, Low)	
	P	S
A. Night school will be very hard on my family.	H	H
B. I'll get bored and stop attending.	L	H
C. It may take longer than 2 years to get the 24 credits I need.	L	M

Now you need to analyze your greatest potential problem by finding likely causes, planning preventive action, and planning contingency action. In solving problems, you act on causes. And to prevent, or be prepared for, potential problems, you look for likely causes. After you have identified the likely causes, ask, "What can be done to reduce the probability that this event (or likely cause) will happen?" In other words, what preventive action can you include in your plans?

But you must also consider: "If the worst comes to pass and the problem does occur, what can I do now to reduce the seriousness of the consequences?" In other words, what contingency action can you include in your plans now?

In the case of Elizabeth, the potential problem "Night school will be very hard on my family" has a high probability of happening; and when it happens, it will be high in seriousness.

6. HIGHEST PRIORITY POTENTIAL PROBLEM

"Night school will be very hard on my family."

LIKELY CAUSES	PREVENTIVE ACTION	CONTINGENCY ACTION
2-nights per week away from family	See if local educational TV station has college courses I can take at home.	Enroll Bill (husband) in one or more courses with me.
Shortage of money	See if organization will pay for all or part. Enroll in state-supported school rather than private college.	Borrow from relatives.
Lack of study time	Buy course books now and start studying in advance. Take courses that are easier for me.	Get family to help me in studying.
Family not aware of hardships	Involve family in pre-planning. Have Bill talk to Joe who is also attending night school.	(No action)

7. REPEAT STEPS 4–6 WITH ANY OTHER CRITICAL
STEP(S)

Elizabeth would then select other critical steps, and repeat Steps 4–
6 by:

- Listing any potential problems concerning each critical step.

- Evaluating each potential problem as to its probability of happening and seriousness if it happens.

- Analyzing each major potential problem for likely causes, preventive action, and contingency action.

The last—and highly important—step in planning is to build your preventive and contingency actions into your original plan at the appropriate points, with completion dates for each action.

In our example, Elizabeth's plan will now look like this:

8. INCORPORATE IMPORTANT PREVENTIVE AND CONTINGENCY ACTIONS INTO YOUR PLAN AT THE APPROPRIATE POINTS.
   A. Have a family meeting to discuss educational
      plans.   Sept. 1
   B. Meet with boss to discuss promotional goal,
      and determine whether the organization
      will assist with tuition.   Sept. 15
   C. Write 3 key development objectives in
      my present job and discuss with boss.   Sept. 30
   D. Meet with college department chairperson
      and identify required and elective courses.
      Consider elective courses that Bill would
      enjoy taking. Also determine at this meeting
      if there are college courses I can take at home. Oct. 15
   E. Analyze my leadership skills; determine my
      strengths and where I need improvement.   Nov. 15
   Etc.

By using this planning process, Elizabeth has greatly increased the probability of reaching her goal. Also note that some of her completion dates have changed in order to include her new activities. At this point (after incorporating the preventive/contingency actions concerning any other high-priority problem), Elizabeth is now able to review her plans to make certain she really can meet her initial objective of being promoted to supervisor within two years.

Many of us spend a great deal of time dealing with a variety of problems, but doing very little planning. We can become so busy running from crisis to crisis that we don't take the time to plan for success—in, or outside, our jobs.

But when you commit yourself to identifying your goals, and follow a proven step-by-step plan to achieve them, you will find you are not sidetracked by problems—and will significantly increase your level of achievement.

On the following pages is a work sheet which will lead you through the eight-step planning process for achieving your major job—and life—objectives.

PLANNING WORK SHEET

After writing down your goals (brainstorming without making judgments), and identifying those with the highest priority, select your most important goal and write it in specific, measurable terms, with a deadline. This is your objective statement.

1. OBJECTIVE: _____
   _____

2. List the steps you should take to achieve this objective, with completion dates.

   STEPS OF PLAN: DATE
   1. _____   _____
   2. _____   _____
   3. _____   _____
   4. _____   _____
   5. _____   _____
   6. _____   _____
   7. _____   _____
   8. _____   _____
   9. _____   _____
   10. _____   _____

3. Analyze which steps have the highest risk of encountering problems. These are critical steps. Mark critical steps with an asterisk or check mark (above list), and then write one of them below. (The following analysis will be later repeated for the other critical steps.)

   CRITICAL STEP: _____
   _____

4. Answer the question, "What can go wrong with this step?" by identifying potential problems.

5. EVALUATE EACH POTENTIAL PROBLEM as to its *probability* of happening, and *seriousness,* if it happens, using H = High, M = Medium, L = Low

POTENTIAL PROBLEMS:	Probability	Seriousness
_____	_____	_____
_____	_____	_____
_____	_____	_____
_____	_____	_____
_____	_____	_____
_____	_____	_____

6. Analyze the highest priority potential problem with likely causes, and prevention and contingency action.

HIGHEST PRIORITY POTENTIAL PROBLEM: _____

LIKELY CAUSES	PREVENTIVE ACTION	CONTINGENCY ACTION

7. REPEAT STEPS 4–6 WITH ANY OTHER CRITICAL STEP(S) using copies of this work sheet.

8. INCORPORATE IMPORTANT PREVENTIVE AND CONTIN-GENCY ACTIONS (from Step 6) as added steps in your original plan (Step 2). Write all steps in logical order, and then number each step. Last, write a completion date for each step.

Step Number	Step	Completion Date
———	———————————————	———
———	———————————————	———
———	———————————————	———
———	———————————————	———
———	———————————————	———
———	———————————————	———
———	———————————————	———
———	———————————————	———
———	———————————————	———
———	———————————————	———
———	———————————————	———
———	———————————————	———
———	———————————————	———
———	———————————————	———
———	———————————————	———
———	———————————————	———
———	———————————————	———
———	———————————————	———
———	———————————————	———

CHAPTER 9
MANAGING YOUR TIME

Remember when we were young, and those lazy summer days stretched on and on? Remember when the closer it got to summer vacation, the longer it took to arrive? Remember when the time from one holiday to the next seemed endless?

And now, why do our days seem hurried, almost mysteriously shortened? What happened? What happened to *time*?

Certainly our perception of time is dependent on what we're doing. We all know how waiting for something we want to happen seems like forever, and how a disagreeable task seems to take so long.

But that's only part of the answer. Our perception of time is also affected by the number of new events we're conscious of in a given period of time. For example, a drive from point A to point B on an unfamiliar road may seem to take forever. But if we travel that same distance on a familiar road, the trip will seem shorter. When we are engaged in habitual tasks, we often wonder at the end of the day where the time has gone. The danger here is that we may not be aware of the way we have managed (or haven't managed) much of this routine time.

Most of us want to become increasingly effective in what we do. But the desire to improve is not all that is necessary. We also need to become aware of how we have been managing our time, so that we are able to understand what positive changes can be made, and why.

Time management is actually a matter of asking yourself some personal questions. The first is: "What are the things that are truly important to me?" Second, "How much of my time am I giving to those things?" And third, "What uses up my time while contributing very little to my goal—or to the quality of my life?"

Time management also means accepting responsibility. It's easy to say, "I have trouble managing my time because—

Other people always interrupt me.
Reports are misfiled by others.
There is too much paper work.
My boss changes his or her priorities.
Others won't cooperate with me.
There are too many emergency project requests.
The computer is always down.
It always seems like I have to wait for others."

Agreed—many of these problems do occur. But they occur to everybody! And we know that some people, facing all of these problems, are much more productive than others.

Good time managers will surely appreciate Reinhold Niebuhr's prayer, "...grant me the serenity to accept the things I cannot change, courage to change the things I can, and the wisdom to know the difference." Effective people have learned to accept the things they can't change, and to take responsibility for the things they can change. And they recognize the difference.

If you are able to exert some control in your life, to make certain decisions, and to accept part of the responsibility for what you do or don't do—then you can do something about your life. And it's *your* choice!

Awareness of Time

Given that you have a positive attitude, that you want to be increasingly effective, and that you are willing to accept responsibility for change, what's next? What are some things you can do to manage your time more productively? First, find out where you are.

Peter Drucker has said, "Memory is treacherous; don't trust it." That is, what you think you did and what you've really done are often two different things. So you must have some way of obtaining accurate data about past actions to use in decisions for future planning. The best method is to use a Time Log to record accurately where you are spending your time.

Reproduce copies of the Time Log on the following page, and use it to record your daily time expenditures. Record *everything* you do. Write down when you are interrupted, and when you interrupt yourself. Note telephone calls, incoming and outgoing; visitors; trips to the water fountain; a coffee break. Write it all down! To obtain enough data for a complete analysis of your time, you should plan to record a minimum of three full days, both at work and at home.

TIME LOG

NAME: _____ DATE: _____

Time	Activity	Time consumed
____	_____	____
____	_____	____
____	_____	____
____	_____	____
____	_____	____
____	_____	____
____	_____	____
____	_____	____
____	_____	____
____	_____	____
____	_____	____
____	_____	____
____	_____	____
____	_____	____
____	_____	____
____	_____	____
____	_____	____
____	_____	____
____	_____	____
____	_____	____
____	_____	____

When you have finished collecting information on how you actually spend your time, add up your time in categories. This will be a major help in determining whether the way you spend your time is really how you want to spend it. Using the following chart, categorize and record each day's information from your Time Log sheets.

	Day 1	Day 2	Day 3	Day 4	Day 5	Day 6	Day 7	TOTAL	%
HOME:									
Yourself	___	___	___	___	___	___	___	___	___
Spouse	___	___	___	___	___	___	___	___	___
Children	___	___	___	___	___	___	___	___	___
Friends	___	___	___	___	___	___	___	___	___
Chores	___	___	___	___	___	___	___	___	___
Eating	___	___	___	___	___	___	___	___	___
Sleeping	___	___	___	___	___	___	___	___	___
Civic	___	___	___	___	___	___	___	___	___
Business	___	___	___	___	___	___	___	___	___
Recreation	___	___	___	___	___	___	___	___	___
Misc.	___	___	___	___	___	___	___	___	___
Home subtotal								___	___
WORK:									
Unscheduled visitors (pleasure)	___	___	___	___	___	___	___	___	___
Unscheduled visitors (business)	___	___	___	___	___	___	___	___	___
Scheduled visitors (pleasure)	___	___	___	___	___	___	___	___	___
Scheduled visitors (business)	___	___	___	___	___	___	___	___	___
Visitors subtotal								___	___
Outgoing telephone (pleasure)	___	___	___	___	___	___	___	___	___
Outgoing telephone (business)	___	___	___	___	___	___	___	___	___
Incoming telephone (pleasure)	___	___	___	___	___	___	___	___	___
Incoming telephone (business)	___	___	___	___	___	___	___	___	___
Telephone subtotal								___	___

Group									
meetings	__	__	__	__	__	__	__	__	__
Waiting	__	__	__	__	__	__	__	__	__
Breaks	__	__	__	__	__	__	__	__	__
Reading	__	__	__	__	__	__	__	__	__
Writing	__	__	__	__	__	__	__	__	__
Faxing	__	__	__	__	__	__	__	__	__
Planning	__	__	__	__	__	__	__	__	__
Physical									
work	__	__	__	__	__	__	__	__	__
Misc.	__	__	__	__	__	__	__	__	__

Total of all categories __ __

After categorizing and recording your Time Log information, determine which time expenditures you wish to change. To do this, you'll need to ask some tough questions, including:

1. Did I use any time to plan for the future?

2. Have I recorded activity—or results? (Activity = what I did. Results = what I accomplished.)

3. What was the longest period of time spent on one thing without interruption?

4. Which interruptions were most costly?

5. What can be done to eliminate or control these interruptions?
   — Which telephone calls were unnecessary?
   — Which phone calls could have been shorter yet equally (or more) effective?
   — Which visits were unnecessary?
   — Which visits could have been shorter yet equally (or more) effective?

6. How much time was spent in meetings?
   — How much was necessary?
   — How could more have been accomplished in less time?

7. Did I find myself jumping from task to task without completing the previous one?

8. Did urgent or crisis work push other things aside?

9. Did I notice a self-correcting tendency occurring as I recorded actions throughout the week?

When you have answered these questions, you are in a much better position to decide what you must change in order to save time in your work and personal life. Of course you may discover that what you do is exactly what you want to do; if so, your final decision will be to do nothing. In either case, the information will help you make the right decision.

And if you make changes, be aware of two points:

1. Increasing the amount of time spent on one activity will require that you take time from another activity.

2. Changes can sometimes cause problems which in turn take even more time to fix.

What is "Urgent"?

Dr. Charles Hummel once wrote an article entitled "The Tyranny of the Urgent." In it he distinguished things that are truly important from those that seem "urgent." When important things and urgent things occur at the same time, which usually wins our attention? Let me give you an example.

A number of years ago, I made the decision to leave the organization I worked for in St. Paul and move my family back to my home state of Virginia. I planned to be my own boss, as an independent training consultant. After a couple of grim years, I finally achieved my bottom line financial goal—i.e., we weren't starving!

At the time, my office was in our converted garage. Because we had many children, I had a business telephone line and a family line.

One Friday evening at about 5:30 we were sitting down for supper when the business line rang. I asked the children to quiet down, and answered the phone. "International Training Consultants—Dick Leatherman speaking. How can I help you?" I said.

The caller was the program director of a local university's management center. He was extremely agitated—so much so I could hardly understand him. Because I was also getting some noise in the kitchen, I put him on hold and went down to the garage to continue the call. "What's wrong?" I asked.

His story was a program director's nightmare. He was at the end of a week-long seminar for about a hundred purchasing agents from up and down the Eastern seaboard. The keynote speaker for Saturday morning was the dean of one of the country's leading law schools. But because the dean had the flu, he wouldn't be there in the morning.

So the program director pleaded, "Dick, will you be our keynote speaker tomorrow morning? We don't care what you do. Just come in and do something!" Let me tell you, that request made me feel good. He had called me first!

But let's put him on hold for a minute so I can tell you about several things I had already scheduled for the Saturday in question.

First, because my office was at home we had some pretty strict rules about the children bothering me when I was working. A week before the program director's call, I had been working in my office when Matthew Leatherman (he was about seven years old at the time) careened in with a big emergency. Well, he wasn't broken or bleeding, and I was irritated that he had interrupted me. As a result I wasn't very nice to him. And as he sulked out of my office, he said under his breath (but just loud enough for me to hear him), "Daddy doesn't have time for me anymore since he has his own business." And Matthew was right. I wasn't spending as much time with him as I once did.

So I said, "Hold it, Bud. You're right. I don't spend as much time with you as I used too. But I'll tell you what—let's me and you have a turtle day next Saturday morning. How about it?" "Oh, yes!" he exclaimed, and I got a big hug.

Do you know what a "turtle day" is? It's when you take a seven-year old boy out to look for turtles. The fact that you probably won't find any is not the point. It's what you can talk about while you look! One-on-one private time between a daddy and his son. That's the point!

And there was another important thing I had scheduled for that Saturday. Laurie, my 16-year old (going on 21), had asked me the preceding Wednesday if I would teach her how to drive. I said, "Hey, honey, my tax dollars help pay for you to get professional driving instruction at your high school! Besides, you don't want to learn my bad driving habits." (I'm a lousy driver.)

"But Daddy," she replied, "I've never driven a car, and I get my 'behind-the-wheel' instructions next week. The other kids will be in the car too, and I don't want to make a fool of myself in front of them!" "Oh, I see," I said. "I'll tell you what—let's spend some time next Saturday at the shopping center parking lot, and you can scare me to death!" "Fantastic!" she said. And I got a big hug for that, too.

The last thing I had scheduled for that Saturday was some time with my youngest daughter, Leanne. Her "Uncle Frank" had made her a giant doll house. It was a marvel to see! It was carpeted, and it had real windows. It also had a low-voltage lighting system with a miniature chandelier hanging in the dining room.

Well, Leanne's house had an attic fire. Somehow the low-voltage wiring had shorted out, and the transformer had burned up. She had been "reminding" me to fix it for a couple of months. And the Tuesday before the Saturday in question, she had asked, "Please, please, please, (or were there four "pleases"?) fix my doll house?" I said, "Tell you what I'm going to do. I'll put the transformer in your doll house this coming Saturday. At the same time, I'll teach you how to solder wires." I got another big hug for that!

Remember, we still have the program director on "hold." What do you think I told him when he frantically said that Friday, "Dick, we don't care what you do. Just come in and do something!" Yes—I said "Okay."

Then I walked up to the kitchen and said, "Guess what, gang? Daddy has a seminar at the Hyatt House tomorrow morning!" There was dead silence. Then my oldest daughter said, "Daddy!" and walked out of the room. Matthew said, "But...but...what about turtle day?" And Leanne, with all the faith and trust of a young child in her father, said, "That's OK, Daddy. I know you'll fix my doll house someday."

I did eventually fix the doll house, go turtle hunting with Matthew, and give Laurie some hints on driving. But not that day—when I let the urgent win out over those things that were truly important to me.

Two lessons can be learned from my experience. First, there is no end to it: the "tyranny of the urgent" is a battle we all will fight day after day. Do you imagine this was the last time I let a crisis get in the way of something that was really important? The thing we must try to do at home and on the job is to choose well when the "urgent" tries to displace the truly **important**.

Second, as Peter Drucker has said, "Learn to say 'no,' nicely if you can but nastily if you must. But learn to say 'no,' so that you have time for the really important things in your life."

If saying no is difficult for you, recognize that you can't say yes to everything. In other words, you have a right to say no. A simple, "No, thank you" is often sufficient and appropriate for those situations where a personal relationship with the other individual is not at issue. And sometimes you will have to say no more than once. Here's an example.

It is 6:30 and you are in the middle of eating supper. The phone rings and you answer it, "Hello?"

Caller: "Is this Ms. Olson?"

You: "Yes."

Caller: "Wonderful! This is William Appleby from the Easy Glide Home Appliance Company. I am happy to inform you that you have won a matching set of stainless steel kitchen knives with genuine molded handles. One of our representatives will be in your area next week to deliver your prize. When would it be convenient for her to stop by?"

You: "Thank you, but I'm really not interested."

Caller: "Ms. Olson, our computer selected you at random for this free set of superb knives that I know you will love having in your home. It won't take but a minute to have them delivered to you. So which would be the best time for you, Monday or Tuesday of next week?"

You: "Thank you, but I'm really not interested."

Caller: "I'm sorry, but I don't understand. Why aren't you interested in owning this free set of fantastic knives?"

You: "Thank you, but I'm really not interested."

At this point, if the caller continues to be a pest, say, "Thank you for calling. Goodbye."—and hang up.

But if a personal relationship with the other person is important to you, first acknowledge the request, then say no, and last add an explanation. For example, suppose you are a great typist. You have a good friend who is taking evening classes at the local college. The conversation goes as follows:

Friend: "Do you have a minute?"

You: "Sure, Jodi. What's up?"

Friend: "I really hate to ask you, but I've got a special paper due Friday. I can't find anybody who can type it for me. Would you mind doing it?"

You: "It sounds like you're facing a tight deadline. I'd really like to help you but I can't. I don't have time to do it."

Friend: "I know you are busy, and I really hate to ask. But you type so fast using your word processer. It's only ten pages. Isn't there some way you could squeeze it in?"

You: "I'm really sorry Jodi, but I can't. I have other plans."

Note that you acknowledged her needs ("It sounds like you're facing a tight deadline"), said "no" tactfully ("I'd really like to help you but I can't"), and gave a reason ("I don't have time to do it"). Note, too, that when your friend persisted in her request, you said "no" again.

But how do you know when to say no? By realizing what is important to you. And how do you ensure that important things are not pushed aside by "urgent" things?

By planning! Planning allows you to identify important goals, and put them into action. The resulting activities generated by this analysis then become a part of your daily planning.

Daily Planning

Daily planning is making a "to-do" list for each day. This list should include the priority items that need to be accomplished immediately, as well as things that you can do today to help carry out your long range goals. It doesn't have to be anything fancy—just a small piece of paper you carry in your pocket or purse to jot down the things you have planned for that (or the next) day. It doesn't make any difference when you do it, whether the first thing in the morning, or at the end of the day. Just so you do it daily!

But keeping a to-do list on a daily basis may involve a significant amount of time. For example, even if you spend only 10 minutes a day making your list, that adds up to about 2,400 minutes—or 40 hours—a year! So there is a cost for doing a daily to-do list. And thus there must be a compelling reason to lead you to do such daily planning.

In fact, there are a number of good reasons why effective people do daily planning. First, when all of the things you feel you need to do today are visibly identified, you can establish your priorities by seeing what's important, and what's only urgent.

Daily planning also helps your supervisor or manager set priorities with you. For example, if your supervisor or manager constantly interrupts you with new crisis requests, it's strategically helpful to be able to hold up a daily to-do list and say, "OK, boss, where does that fit on my list?"

Third, a to-do list acts as a memory aid. I, for one, have reached an age where if I don't write it down, there is only a very small chance I'll remember what it was that I said I absolutely wouldn't forget!

I use a daily to-do list for yet another reason. It tells me what to do next after finishing a task. I am a very task-oriented person. While I'm working on a task, I usually don't think of other things that need to be done. Then when I finish a job, because I can't think of what I wanted to do next, I may simply take a break. But if I have a to-do list in front of me, I can see exactly what I need to do next.

Others who keep daily to-do lists report that it simply feels good to scratch tasks off their list as they are completed. In other words, you have set up a way of giving yourself immediate positive feedback as each task is completed.

Finally, I save my lists for a month or so and review them to see if I can discover any ways that I can further improve my time management. For example, if I haven't completed a task that I had planned to do that day, I immediately rewrite that task on the next day's list. And if I see that I rewrote a particular task more than once, I realize that I may be procrastinating.

If you don't now use a daily to-do list, try it! It will be time well invested. Or simply commit yourself to keeping a list for 20 working days. When you see that it pays off, you will continue to use such a list without difficulty, because you've gotten into the "to-do habit."

On the next page is one example of a to-do list. Make as many copies as needed. Then stack the sheets and staple at the top to make your own to-do pads.

Summary

We have presented several concrete strategies for managing your time well:

- Time logs
- Prioritizing important things over "urgent" ones
- Daily planning with "to-do lists"

Using these techniques will allow you to accomplish key tasks on schedule—and have more time for creative thinking, for your boss, and for yourself. To become a better manager of your time, you need to spend it on those things that are really important. In short, you need to take control of your life!

MANAGING YOUR TIME

Tasks to Do	Priority	Time

CHAPTER 10
MANAGING YOUR
PERFORMANCE APPRAISAL

INTRODUCTION

Background. Some years ago I had a boss who was truly incompetent in conducting performance appraisals. To compound the problem, he had no idea that he didn't know how to handle employee appraisal meetings. The result of his brief once-a-year session was that I felt bad about him, and about the organization I worked for. And most importantly, I felt bad about me!

But I knew that his short annual presentation of my strengths and weaknesses was a poor way to conduct a performance appraisal. Since that time, I have read everything I could on the topic of performance appraisal. I have also attended numerous workshops on this subject, conducted appraisal sessions with many employees, talked to thousands of managers, supervisors, and employees, and taught hundreds of workshops on this topic.

And only now, some thirty-five years after my first unfortunate experiences, do I feel comfortable—most of the time—participating in a performance appraisal session. I have learned a lot, and much of it the hard way!

What's in this section. Following is a step-by-step approach for you to use in *managing* your performance appraisal interviews. This planned approach will help you provide your supervisor or manager with better information in order to help him or her conduct a productive, balanced, and fair performance appraisal session with you.

This method is *not* a "sit-back-and-listen-as-your-boss-tells-you-your-strengths-and-weaknesses" approach. It is *participative*. But there is a cost to you. It requires you to spend time preparing for your appraisal meeting. You will find, as a result, that the appraisal interview will run longer—to your advantage. There may also be more open disagreements during your meeting. But an open discussion will allow you and your leader to arrive at a true understanding of your actual performance.

PLANNING FOR THE REVIEW

Sometimes we run into problems in our performance appraisal interviews because we don't know clearly what is expected of us. "I didn't know that I was supposed to do that!" many of us have said. In addition, most of us have asked questions such as, "What is a good job?" or, "When am I not doing this job well enough?" And, "When am I devoting too much time and energy to this task?" These questions indicate that someone hasn't explained what is expected of us during the period being appraised.

Analyzing your job. To avoid such problems, plan to meet with your boss six to twelve months ahead of time to discuss your specific job responsibilities. By making copies of and filling out the following job analysis work sheet, you will be prepared to discuss and obtain agreement on your job tasks with your supervisor or manager.

JOB ANALYSIS WORK SHEET

List the main tasks of your job.	How critical is each job task? "A"=Highest "B"=Medium "C"=Lowest	What standards are used to measure your job performance?	What problems exist which handicap your performance?	Authority levels*		
				1	2	3

*A "#1 authority level" means that you, the employee, have total authority to perform the task. In other words, you don't have to ask permission to do the task, or even tell your boss that you did it. You simply do it because it's a routine part of your job. A "#2 authority level" allows you to perform the task without first asking for permission. But you are expected to let your boss know that you did it. A "#3 authority level" indicates that you need to obtain approval from your boss before doing that task.

Fill out the work sheet on the previous page. Then meet to discuss it with your manager. You are likely to be amazed at the number of times the two of you do not agree about which tasks are most important, the standards for tasks, and the authority you have for each task. And you will find that this meeting will help greatly to ensure that your efforts are on track. Your next performance appraisal meetings will be more fair and productive as a result.

Reminder file. It will also be helpful for you to keep a performance appraisal reminder file throughout the year. When you complete a special project or do a job well, make a note of this and place it in your file. Similarly, when you have problems with a task, figure out what happened, and write it up for your file. Then when you are preparing for your next performance appraisal session, you will have accurate information to use in doing a candid self-assessment. (See the interview form found at the end of this chapter.)

PREPARING FOR THE PERFORMANCE APPRAISAL INTERVIEW

An effective performance appraisal interview requires that you and your supervisor spend quality time talking about your past performance, areas for improvement, and ways to make your strengths even better. Too often this does not happen. If such a discussion is important to you, you may need to take the initiative to prepare yourself for the interview.

The organization's system. If your organization has a poor appraisal system, you may have difficulty changing it. But there *are* important things you can do—things that will not only help you receive a fair and constructive appraisal interview, but will also help your boss and the organization as well.

For example, suppose your organization expects your supervisor to present you with your completed appraisal, giving you little or no opportunity for input. An effective way of solving this problem is to ask your boss to conduct an informal appraisal interview with you every three months, as well as shortly *before* the "official" appraisal session. This will not only produce an interview that is fairer to you, but will give your boss better information to use when he or she is later required to fill out the appraisal form.

If your boss feels a need to stay with an out-of-date company policy regulation that requires that you simply be presented with your appraisal, then don't count this as an "informal performance appraisal meeting." Simply label it something else. Most leaders, for example, will be happy to schedule a private meeting with you in order to "review your job performance."

On the other hand, suppose that your organization's performance appraisal system is great, but your supervisor's approach isn't. For example, if your boss spent only a few minutes conducting your last appraisal interview, the first thing you need to do is to let him or her know ahead of time that you are preparing in advance for your next interview, and would appreciate at least an hour of uninterrupted time for it.

Your responsibility. Next, prepare carefully. If you don't have a copy of the performance appraisal form that your organization uses, find one. Then look it over to become familiar with its layout. Assess the kinds of information requested. Most appraisal forms list general duties, personality traits, and work habits, and rate you on them. Other forms are customized for your specific job, and ratings are assigned for each of your major job duties. (This is the better type of form.)

Whatever kind of form your organization uses, it will normally ask the rater to analyze your strengths and the areas needing improvement. This is where you will be doing most of your preparation. The idea is for *you* to be thoroughly prepared to discuss both your strengths and areas of need. And if you have a participative supervisor, he or she will appreciate your preparation because it will make his or her job that much easier.

One word of caution. It is best not to plan to discuss salary, promotion, or your career path in this meeting. It is very difficult to discuss honestly your past, present, and future performance if, at the same time, you are looking for a promotion or salary increase. It is far better to concentrate on your performance at this meeting, and set up another meeting at a later time to discuss a salary increase or promotion.

What you do. Here are the steps to follow in preparing for your performance appraisal interview:

1. If you don't know when your next appraisal interview is scheduled, find out. Otherwise you may find yourself surprised by your boss walking up to your desk and saying, "I'd like to see you in my office at ten o'clock this morning for your annual performance appraisal interview." You need to learn when your interview is scheduled so that you will have sufficient time to prepare for it. If you aren't given an exact date, try to determine an approximate one.

2. If you don't have a blank copy of your organization's performance appraisal form (or a copy of your appraisal the previous year), get one and look it over. Don't fill it out at this point. Simply review it to determine what information is needed.

3. Next, list the major duties of your job, and evaluate the tasks that represent your strengths and the areas where you need to improve.

4. Look at each of your job strengths to see if there is any way this skill could be even further developed. Also look to see if any of your strengths are not being fully used by your organization at the present time. If this is so, develop any strategies that will better match your strengths to the needs of your department or section.

5. Then examine the job areas where you feel your performance needs to be improved. Your first task is to analyze, for each need area, *why* unsatisfactory results are occurring (or satisfactory results are not occurring). When you feel you understand the causes of any problems, try to develop possible solutions.

6. If your organization's performance appraisal form requires noting personality traits and/or job habits, be sure also to analyze them in order to determine your strengths and needs. Although these may not be directly related to job performance, improvements in job habits and/or personality traits often help us to become more effective.

7. Write out brief action plans for improving your performance in the areas of both your strengths and needs. These action plans will be tentative at this point, since you will be asking your boss later for his or her evaluation and ideas for improving them.

8. Now, using the information from Steps 3 through 7 above, fill out the form yourself. This will help you prepare by allowing you to see better how your boss may approach your meeting, and how he or she may perceive you.

9. If you know that your organization's performance appraisal system will not allow you to provide input during the actual interview, then ask your supervisor for a one-hour private meeting to informally discuss your "job performance." If your boss normally conducts such interviews in his or her office, where interruptions are a problem, ask if he or she would be

willing to reserve a conference room or some other location where you can have privacy.

Then the day before this job performance meeting, remind your boss that it is scheduled for the next day, and that you are looking forward to it. (Supervisors and managers, like others, sometimes forget meetings that they didn't initiate.)

MANAGING YOUR PERFORMANCE APPRAISAL INTERVIEW

Your goal in your performance appraisal interview is to actively guide the discussion along the most helpful channels without being offensive. If you do all of the talking, you will not be able to take advantage of your boss's suggestions, ideas and advice. On the other hand, if you allow your boss to do all of the talking, he or she will not have the opportunity to learn important things from, and about, you. The best strategy is to maintain a balance between these two extremes. In a participative performance appraisal session, a good guideline might be for you to talk about 60% of the time, and your supervisor or manager about 40%.

Please note that the step-by-step plan that follows requires that you be honest—honest with yourself, and honest with your boss. You will find it fairly easy to be honest when discussing your strengths. But it may be a lot harder to maintain equal honesty when discussing areas in which you need to improve!

It is important for you to level with your boss in discussing areas of needed improvement. For one thing, if you present only your strengths, you will lose control of the interview when your boss brings your "weaknesses" up for discussion. It is far better for you to present your areas of need than to make your boss do so because you have not.

Secondly, if you don't bring up problem areas for discussion, you communicate that you don't trust your boss's ability to react. Also, you will not appear to have an objective view of yourself (we all can improve), or the capacity for self-criticism needed for growth. And if you don't bring up problem areas, and your boss also fails to do so, how are you going to get ideas for improvement?

A good balance between speaking and listening, with honesty, is not easy to attain—especially without a plan. But with a well-conceived step-by-step approach you can achieve this balance.

Step-by-step approach. The following outline will help you to manage your performance appraisal interview with fair, constructive, and profitable results for all concerned.

1. Introduction.

   Greet your supervisor or manager and tell him or her how pleased you are to have this opportunity to meet and discuss your performance. Thank him or her for the uninterrupted time that has been set aside for the meeting, and also for the time that he or she may have spent in preparation.

2. Agree to the objectives for this meeting.

   Ask your manager or supervisor what he or she sees are the major objectives for this meeting.

   Next ask if you could first:
   - present your thoughts on your strengths and achievements
   - present your view of areas where you need additional improvement

- discuss your tentative action plans for improving your performance in specific areas
- secure his or her reaction, ideas and suggestions about these plans

Then ask if he or she would help you:

- gain further feedback on the areas of strength and need that you did not mention
- obtain help in setting priorities on the things that need to be done as a result of the meeting

3. Present your topics for discussion.
- First, present one of your strengths.
  — Describing the strength, using specific examples.

Example: Don't simply state, "First, I'd like to mention my success in organizing my work."

Better to say, "First, I'd like to discuss my ability to organize my work. For example, several months ago, I spent a lot of time analyzing my work flow. Based on that analysis I established a new system of prioritizing each job I receive. This has helped reduce the amount of time I have had to spend on 'fire-fighting,' and has allowed me to manage my work much more productively."

— Next, present your tentative action plan for even better utilizing this strength.

Example: You might say, "Here are some ideas I have on how I can further organize my work."

— Then, solicit ideas for better utilization of this strength.

Example: "What suggestions do you have for using my organizational ability to even better advantage?"

Or, "How can I be even more productive in this area?"

— Finally, discuss any ideas that have emerged, and arrive at an agreement.

Follow this same format in discussing other important areas of strength. However, due to time constraints it would be wise to select only a few of your major strengths for this initial meeting.

- Next, identify an area of work where you wish to improve your performance.
    - Describe what is happening in this area in specific terms. Use examples to illustrate the problem if possible.

Example: "I find that I am constantly interrupted. Some of the interruptions are related to my job; but some aren't. As a result, I find that I don't get as much done as I would like. During this past week, for example, I kept an 'interruption list.' By the end of the week, I found that I had been interrupted an average of 11 times per day, and only about 40% of the interruptions were work-related."

— Describe what you want to happen. Again, be specific, avoiding general statements if possible.

Example: "I am not sure what is 'normal.' But I think if I could reduce the non-work-related interruptions by at least 50%, I can be a lot more effective."

— State what you feel is the cause (or causes) of the problem.

Example: "I studied my log to see if I could find any patterns. And interestingly enough, I saw that one individual accounted for an average of 2 interruptions per day. And there were at least 2 other interruptions a day from people who wanted to borrow items from me. So I see two causes. One cause is an employee who likes to talk, and I don't say no. And the other cause concerns my desk. My desk seems to be the local supply cabinet! I got interrupted twice for aspirin, and once for 3-M Post-its. Someone else needed to borrow my extra stamp pad, another person wanted a blue-line proofing pencil, and a third person asked for a formated 3 1/2" disk."

— Describe your suggested solution(s).

Example: "As I see it, there are two things I can do. First is to stop being the local supply cabinet. I'll clean out my desk, put extra supplies back in the supply room, and let everybody know what I've done.

"Dealing with the individual who is interrupting me the most will be more difficult. She is going through a separation from her husband, and needs to talk to somebody—and it looks like I've been elected! I want to help by being there for her; but it has resulted in a major problem for me. What I would like to do is be straight with her about my job needs and suggest that we meet for lunch, or talk at break times. The thing I don't want to do is have her think that nobody cares."

— Describe your tentative action plan, if pertinent.

(In the example above, it is probably not necessary to have a full-blown action plan, since most of the solutions seem to be fairly obvious.)

— Ask for feedback on your plans, and additional suggestions.

Example: "What do you think?" or, "What other ideas do you have?"

— Discuss suggestions and arrive at a consensus.

— Present any other important areas of needed improvement following the same format. Again, due to time limitations, you may wish to select only a few key areas to discuss.

4. Request information about areas of strength or need that you have not already mentioned.

- Ask: "What other strengths or needed improvement do you feel we should discuss that I haven't mentioned?"

Here, it is very important that you not become defensive when your boss brings up an area, or areas, where he or she feels you need to improve. It may be difficult—but listen; don't interrupt. Don't mentally prepare your response. Instead, ask questions. Ask for examples to help your supervisor or manager explain his or her viewpoint. Again, do not become upset about seemingly "negative" feedback. You are not being attacked! Remember that your boss is trying to help you by offering suggestions for improvement—which you have just asked for.

5. Prioritize the topics that have been discussed.

If a number of different strengths and areas for improvement have been discussed, it may be necessary to prioritize them, for two reasons. First, implementing new solutions and plans will require a significant amount of time. But you may not have enough time to handle all of the needed changes immediately. Second, you and your supervisor or manager may need to agree on which action plan is most important—which one should be implemented first.

6. Establish dates for a follow-up meeting.

In your follow-up meeting, you will discuss the progress you have made in implementing your plan(s) for improvement, and discuss any additional problems that may be occurring as a result of the changes you have made.

7. Thank your supervisor or manager for his or her time and suggestions.

Following is a planning work sheet that uses the above approach. It will help you outline the steps you will follow in your performance appraisal interview. The experience of many employees and supervisors indicates that this time-tested approach will prove to be both productive and rewarding.

MANAGING YOUR PERFORMANCE APPRAISAL INTERVIEW

Write below what you plan to say during the interview. Do not write a word-for-word "script," but only your notes indicating what you want to say at each step of the interview.

1. **Introduction**

   Greeting: _____

   _____

   Express your appreciation: _____

   _____

2. **Agree to the objectives for this meeting**

   _____

   _____

   _____

   _____

   _____

3. **Present your topics for discussion**

   A. Describe a key strength: _____

   _____

   Example(s) of this strength: _____

   _____

   Present your tentative action plan for even better utilizing this strength (if applicable): _____

   _____

   _____

   _____

   _____

   _____

Solicit ideas for better utilization of this strength. Write the question you will ask: _____

_____

    Record suggested ideas: _____

    _____

    _____

    _____

    Discuss suggestions, and arrive at a consensus.
    Record your agreement: _____

    _____

    _____

    _____

    _____

If you have more than one strength to present, duplicate these pages and continue this step until completed.

    B.   Present for discussion an area of your work in which you feel you need to improve your performance.
         Describe what has been happening, in specific terms:

         _____

         _____

         _____

         _____

         Note examples: _____

         _____

         _____

         Describe what you want to happen. Again, be specific:

         _____

         _____

         _____

         _____

State what you feel is the cause (or causes) of the problem:

_____
_____
_____
_____

Describe your suggested solution(s):

_____
_____
_____
_____

Describe any tentative action plan(s) you may have:

_____
_____
_____
_____
_____
_____

Ask for feedback on your plan(s), and additional suggestions. Indicate the question you will ask: _____

_____

Record reactions and suggestions: _____

_____
_____
_____

Discuss suggestions, and arrive at consensus. Record your agreement: _____

_____
_____

If you have more than one area of need to present, duplicate these pages and continue this step until completed.

4. **Request additional information about areas of strength or need that you have not already mentioned**

Indicate question you will ask: _____

_____

_____

Note strengths that are mentioned (with suggestions for utilizing them even better, if they are given): _____

_____

_____

Note areas needing improvement that are mentioned: _____

_____

_____

_____

What examples illustrate this concern? _____

_____

_____

_____

How should you be performing? _____

_____

_____

_____

What does your manager feel is the cause of the situation? _____

_____

_____

What do you feel is the cause of the situation? _____

_____

_____

What solutions, or suggestions, does your manager have? _____

_____

_____

What other solutions do you see? _____

_____

_____

Describe your action plan(s) below:

_____

_____

_____

_____

_____

_____

_____

_____

_____

Make several copies of pages 175–76 to take with you into the interview (i.e., one for each area of needed improvement that might be suggested).

5. **Prioritize the topics that have been discussed**

   List below (one line if possible) each of the topics discussed during the meeting:

   Topic   Priority

   _____   _____

   _____   _____

   _____   _____

   _____   _____

   _____   _____

   _____   _____

   _____   _____

   _____   _____

   _____   _____

   Looking over the above topics with your manager, jointly assign priorities to those topics (areas for improvement, strengths) that need follow-up action. (i.e., which should be addressed first, which second, and so forth. Or, which is most important, next most important, etc.).

6. **Establish dates for a follow-up meeting**

   Indicate how you will ask for a follow-up meeting: _____

   _____

   When will be a good time for you? _____

   Tentative follow-up date: _____

7. **Thank your supervisor or manager for his or her time and suggestions**

   Indicate what you will say: _____

   _____

   _____

   _____

   _____

   _____

CHAPTER 11
IT'S *YOUR* CAREER

In the preceding chapters, I have made a strong case for the need to accept personal responsibility in managing your performance appraisal interview, your time, your attitude—each part of your job life. And this is also true in managing your career development. Your organization is not responsible for your career. Your boss is not responsible for your career. You are!

INTRODUCTION

At the turn of the century, an entire generation of young people grew up reading a series of novels written by Horatio Alger. The books had titles like *Strive and Succeed, Making His Way, Struggling Upward, Do and Dare*, and *Helping Himself.*

In almost every case these books had a plot that went something like this: A young boy had either an absent father, or a father (usually a minister) who was kind and good, but was not concerned with the practical side of life. The family was always poor, and there was usually a rich villain who was going to foreclose on the mortgage—a princely sum like $500, in a day when you could buy a house for $600.

But the ending always turned out happily. Happily, in the Horatio Alger stories, meant that the boy earned the money to pay the mortgage because he was honest, hardworking, kind, and loved God, his mother, and his country. The central theme was: "If you are willing to work hard, success will come automatically because of the grand opportunities that exist in this country."

Today, the Horatio Alger story is, unfortunately, largely untrue. This is so because the facts of life in the business world are quite changed. We still view the individual as fundamentally responsible for his or her success or failure. But the maxim "Hard work will ensure success" has by now become more myth than truth. Look at the facts. In the 1950's and 60's, the chances of being promoted were one in five. Today the odds are one in thirty. In other words, you are six times less likely to be promoted today than you would have been in the recent past.

Future expectations are formed by past experiences. A whole generation—our parents—grew up with remarkable opportunities. So we, their children, have similarly high expectations. We were told, "Work hard. Stay in school. Go to college. Get your degree. Do these things, and you will succeed!" As a result, we expect responsible jobs with opportunities for advancement. But we will not find the same opportunities as they did in the past.

Developing a career plan, either with the help of your organization or on your own, can help you overcome obstacles and achieve success.

CAREER DEVELOPMENT SYSTEMS

Good organizations know that their employees are their strength. Today you will find such organizations helping employees build careers to become more and more valuable to the organization. On the next page is a picture of the way the parts of a modern career system fit together. As you can see, the central focus is on career counseling and career action plans.

Organizational Strategies

Organizations are built on a foundation of strategic planning. This planning is usually conducted by top management in order to define

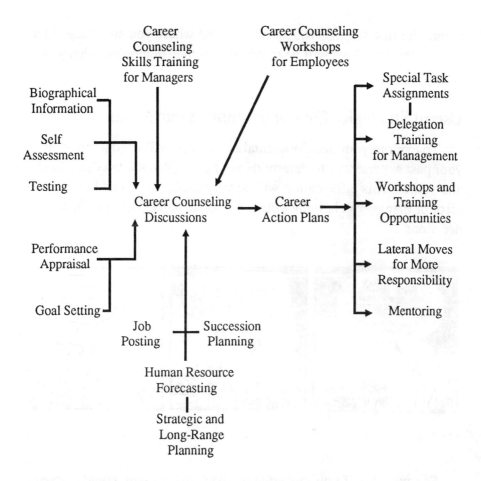

the organization's mission or vision. From the organization's definition of what it is about—its vision and mission—a long-range plan is
developed.

After the organization does long-range planning, it can then fore-
cast its human resource needs. When the forecasting is complete, the
organization can then do succession planning to determine who needs
to be trained to do what in future jobs. Then the organization communicates its human resource needs to its employees by job-posting.

But even if your organization does not do forecasting or succession planning, you can still take responsibility for your career develop-

ment. The first step for you is to figure out where you are going, what knowledge and skills will be required, and then determine what you need to do to get there.

Useful Strategies for Determining Your Needs

To explore your developmental needs, you will need to analyze your past experiences to determine your strengths, knowledge, skills, and values. This information will be very useful to you and your supervisor or manager in helping you make sound career development decisions.

For example, if you looked at my background you would discover that in almost every job I have had, I've enjoyed making presentations. Even in high school, my only A was in Public Speaking. (Where I went to school, it was socially unacceptable to make too many A's.) Therefore, if you were assisting me with my career planning, you would focus on my strength of being able to make presentations.

Job History form. One way to organize information about yourself is to fill out a "Job History" form. To fill out a copy of this form (found at the end of this chapter), begin by listing each job you have held in the past, starting with your present job (maximum of 5). A major job change within one organization is counted as a new job.

Next, break each job down into its major tasks. Enter the details on the form. Then show your personal level of satisfaction for each task. Finally, for those tasks rated highest or lowest in satisfaction, note the reasons why you liked or disliked each task. This list will provide themes and clues to the key things you want in a career, as well as the things you wish to avoid.

The following is an example of a job history for one of my past positions:

JOB HISTORY

1. Job	2. Major tasks	3. Satisfaction 5 = High Level 1 = Low Level	4. Why did you like or dislike this specific task?
	Team Leader	3	
	Long Range Planning	4	
	Handling Budgets	1	I hate dealing with budgets because I am
	Writing and Creating New Programs	3	not very good at it!
	Making Presenta-tions to Executives	2	
	Acting as Resource Person for Technical Questions	5	I enjoy being the "expert" and helping people.
	Speaking at Local and National Conventions	5	The recognition I receive feels good to me. I also like being competent.

5. **What generalizations (themes) can you make about yourself from your job history analysis? What are the key things you want in a job, and what things do you wish to avoid?**
   1. I like the mentoring role.

   2. Recognition for work well done is important to me.

   3. I would strongly dislike working with numbers.

Life History form. In addition to the Job History form, you should also fill out a copy of a "Life History" form (found at the end of this chapter). This form also asks you to identify major skills and interests.

To use this form, first list five key positive events that have occurred in your life, either job-related or personal, that resulted mostly from your own efforts. Then, for each event list the skills or abilities you used that produced the positive experience.

Next, honestly indicate specific reasons why each of the events was important to you. Then examine each of your skills and abilities, and make a new list of the most important ones. Finally, as a result of analyzing the reasons why each positive event was personally important, list the underlying values that were shown in that event. That is, list what you liked and enjoyed about each situation.

To illustrate the use of this form, take as an example a life event that was significant to me. The teachers in my elementary school thought I was "strange." I could read at an astonishing speed. But I absolutely could not spell. As a matter of fact, after failing the sixth grade I almost became a grammar school dropout.

It wasn't until I was in college that I learned I had a condition referred to as "dyslexia." Many years later I felt honored when I was asked to give the commencement address to a special high school graduating class of 12 students—who were all dyslexic! The next page shows the way I wrote up this positive event.

It is difficult to perceive the power of these two forms until you have had an opportunity to experience them. At the end of this chapter there is a set of both forms to copy and fill out concerning yourself.

TESTING

There are a number of tests, or questionnaires, that can help you to determine your career interests or needs. Examples of such tests are John Holland's *Self-Directed Search,* the Myers-Briggs *Type*

LIFE HISTORY

1. Positive event	2. List your skills/abilities that resulted in this event	3. Why was this event importamt to you?
I gave the commencement address to a high school class of dyslexics	— Speaking before groups — Writing skills (not spelling!) — Knowledge of how to conduct a needs assessment (I interviewed each of the 12 students prior to writing the speech)	— Recognition; I felt needed — Satisfaction in helping others personally

4. From #2 above, list your most important skills and abilities	5. Identify your underlying values
Speaking before groups	— I like being in a situation where I can help others and am perceived as being exceptional — I enjoy the resulting recognition

Indicator, and, for supervisory or management positions, the *Leatherman Leadership Questionnaire.* Tests such as these can usually be obtained through your organization's personnel department.

There are two main kinds of tests to help people determine career interests and needs. The more common tests are called "perception" questionnaires. "Knowledge-based" questionnaires are less common.

Perception questionnaires. These tests are used to determine which of a list of topics are perceived as being career development needs. For example, a questionnaire that begins by asking an employee, "Which of the following topics do you feel are important for your future development?" belongs in this class of test.

Perception tests are easy and quick to complete. They can be filled out by the person being tested, the boss, or a peer.

Unfortunately, perception tests also have very serious limitations. For example, some topics from a career development test may be selected as critical when, in fact, they may not be needs at all. If topics such as "communications," or "time management" appear in a list, they are almost guaranteed to be selected as critical. This is because they are what we call umbrella terms.

In other words, terms like "communications" and "time management" are labels that cover a number of different subtopics. If any sub-parts are really important to you, you will mark "time management" as important. But other parts may not be important to you at all.

Also, what people think they need, and what they really need, may be quite different. For example, you may have little competence in managing your performance appraisal interviews, and not know that you need help in this area. This often happens when your supervisor or manager doesn't know how to interview either. In fact, entire organizations often don't know that they don't know how to conduct performance appraisals effectively!

Knowledge-based questionnaires. These tests, on the other hand, are used to determine our actual knowledge in specific areas. For example, a typical knowledge-based question would look like the following:

The primary responsibility for career development rests with the:

A. Employee's immediate supervisor.

B. Personnel department's establishment of career development programs and procedures (e.g., mentoring, training programs, career planning systems).

C. Employee.

D. Chief executive of the organization, since his or her support is essential for the success of any career development program.

Like perception tests, knowledge-based tests are easy to administer. But unlike perception tests, knowledge-based tests provide very accurate information if they are properly developed. Also, they tell exactly what the person knows, rather than what he or she thinks.

Assessment centers. Another testing strategy that is used by some large organizations to determine career development needs is called an "assessment center." An assessment center uses a several-day process with trained observers to rate employees as they complete a variety of simulated tasks.

For example, each assessor observes participants for one to five days as they participate in group discussions, work individually on special assignments, give presentations, solve problems, and make decisions.

Assessment centers have proved to be a valid and reliable way of finding employee developmental needs. In addition, the feedback given to the employees at the end of the assessment period is usually quite helpful.

But assessment centers place heavy stress on the people tested. And they cost a lot to run, even though they test only small groups of people.

PERFORMANCE APPRAISAL SYSTEMS

Another source that can help identify your needs and strengths is a performance appraisal—when it is done properly (see Chapter 10). If your leader is honest and accurate in his or her feedback to you, if the appraisal system is designed to allow you to be a part of the discussion, and if the performance appraisal form includes information about your future, then good career development information can be obtained.

But in order for the performance appraisal interview to be meaningful for you—and the organization—you must have an opportunity well in advance to discuss your job responsibilities with your supervisor or manager (as much as one year prior to the interview, if possible). This type of interview is important in order to reduce the chances that you will later be appraised on things you should have done but didn't. Here, there should be a full discussion of the job's tasks, the standards for each task, your authority level for the task, and a careful analysis of any problems that might impede your performance.

In addition, your manager or supervisor must be able to give you honest and straightforward feedback in appraising you. Managers and supervisors must also be willing to spend time in the appraisal interview discussing not only your past and present performance, but your future as well. And last, the performance appraisal form itself should address such issues as career planning and setting future developmental goals and objectives.

As a part of a complete performance management system, some organizations use a formal goal-setting process where you, with your leader's help, write job-related goals and objectives, and then create a plan to reach each objective. This type of information, even though it is aimed at your present job tasks, can provide further career development data.

CAREER DEVELOPMENT WORKSHOPS

Most performance appraisal systems fall short of the desired standard. Therefore, many organizations have helped the employee accept responsibility for his or her own career development by setting up career development workshops for them. In these workshops the employees complete work sheets much like the "Job History" and "Life History" forms presented earlier, and design action plans for their personal development.

Such workshops will not only assist you in identifying your knowledge, skills, and values, but will also let you know that you are not alone in your career development needs. A payoff for the organization is that employees often find that they have far better opportunities within their organization than outside of it.

MANAGER-EMPLOYEE CAREER COUNSELING SESSIONS

One of the best ways your supervisor or manager can help you with your career development is to help you with career planning. He or she can help you to:

1. Determine whether your organizational goals are realistic.

2. Identify your strengths and determine whether those strengths are important for future positions.

3. Identify areas of needed improvement.

4. Communicate career job alternatives.

5. Create action plans for continued development covering both strengths and needs.

Now let's look at some important strategies to guide you in your career counseling session.

THE CAREER COUNSELING INTERVIEW

In this section we will explain an eight-step procedure for participating in a career counseling session with your manager or supervisor, describing each step in detail. The eight key steps are as follows:

1. Prepare for the meeting.

2. Open the interview.

3. Present your perceptions of your knowledge, skills, and values.

4. Ask for feedback on your perceptions.

5. Explore career choice alternatives.

6. Create an action plan.

7. Conclude the interview.

8. Follow up.

1. Prepare for the Meeting

Make an appointment with your leader. Not only should you prepare for your career counseling meeting, but your supervisor or manager should do so as well. Therefore, briefly meet with your leader and ask him or her for a one-hour appointment in about two to three weeks' time. Tell him or her that you would like to discuss your career goals and get some ideas on the kinds of developmental activities you should undertake. Ask him or her to think about any special jobs or tasks that would be appropriate for you, particular training opportunities that might exist, and also ways of making your present job more challenging.

Tell your leader that you will make every effort to be honest about areas of needed improvement, as well as strengths; but that you would like feedback and help as well. Inform your manager or supervisor that your objectives are to determine:

- whether or not your career goals are realistic.

- what the organization needs in the future and how you can best contribute to those needs.

- what skills are required for these future positions.

In addition, tell him or her that you will bring to the meeting an analysis of your own job and life skills and interests as well as a tentative action plan for reaching your career goals.

Fill out the Job and Life History forms. After setting a meeting date with your supervisor or manager, fill out both the Job History and Life History forms. These forms will help you to identify your knowledge, skills, and abilities, and also enable you to determine the kinds of things you really enjoy doing, as well as those you don't.

Use the Job History form to list five jobs or positions you've held in the past, starting with your present job and working backward. Use the Life History form to list significant events in your experience.

Develop alternative career goals. Next, consider your talents and skills, as well as the things you like and don't like doing, and decide where you want to be in the future. Within reason, the more alternative career goals you bring to your counseling session to examine, the better your decisions will be. This means looking ahead at many possibilities, including job enrichment in your present job, special projects, or lateral moves for more exposure or challenge.

A good strategy is to brainstorm a list of possible career goals. The idea is to create a list of goals on paper without judging the possibility they can be achieved. When your list is complete, delete those goals that seem impractical, combine the remaining ones where possible, and even add to the list new ideas that come to mind.

Create a career plan. When you have identified the direction you would like to go (even tentatively), begin to develop a step-by-step plan to reach your goal. A Career Goal Planning Work Sheet is found at the end of this chapter. Make several copies of this work sheet for use in your planning.

As an example of step-by-step planning, you may recall that I moved from a corporate job to my own consulting firm. In planning this career change, I wrote the following plan:

		Date to be Completed
1.	Discuss with spouse.	January 15
2.	Analyze my salable strengths.	January 16
3.	Take a week's vacation and determine market potential by meeting confidentially with ten key potential clients in Virginia.	February 1
4.	Meet with several other key successful consultants. Ask each one, "If I do this, what can go wrong?"	February 1
5.	Determine equipment that will be needed.	February 15
6.	Project yearly business and family expenses.	February 25
7.	Locate resource people (i.e., CPA/bookkeeper, attorney, banker)	March 15
8.	Locate source of funds.	April 15
9.	Give notice at work.	May 1
10.	Select a replacement for my job.	May 15
11.	Select ten key accounts and visit them for an analysis of their needs.	June 1
12.	Design a mailing for all prospective clients and announce my availability.	July 1
13.	Follow up mail responses with phone calls and meetings where appropriate.	

Analyzing risk. Notice the key question in Step 4 of my plan: "If I do this, what can go wrong?" This is an important question you need to ask yourself, and others, as you prepare your plan. The idea is to try to develop preventive and contingency actions you can take if problems occur. Preventive action includes those things you can do now to reduce the probability a problem will occur. Contingency action is what you will do to stabilize your plan if the problem occurs anyway.

You may wish to develop several tentative career plans for your meeting with your supervisor or manager. One is your primary plan. The others can be used if your primary plan proves to be unrealistic for your organization.

Your career plan is tentative at this point. To implement a plan, it must meet not only your needs, but the organization's needs as well.

2. Open the interview

The day of your interview with your supervisor or manager has arrived. Take paper and pencil, your completed Job History and Life History forms, and your Career Goal Planning Work Sheet. You will probably feel a little nervous. But this is natural—and in any case you are prepared. You have done considerable thinking and organized planning, and committed it to writing to make your discussion easier. In other words, you have done your homework and are prepared to take charge of your meeting.

3. Present your perceptions of your knowledge, skills, and values

Now you will begin the process of giving important personal information to your supervisor or manager. A good way to start is to summarize your strengths highlighted in your Job History form, and indicate the types of tasks that have been satisfying and dissatisfying to you. Then you will turn to your Life History form and review your knowledge, skills, and values. (Summarize your findings by reviewing only the most important events, skills and abilities, and values.)

4. Ask for feedback on your perceptions

At this point you will need to stop talking, and listen. Ask your supervisor or manager how he or she feels about your analysis. What else should be added, both in the areas of strengths and needs?

You must not become defensive if your boss gives some feedback that seems uncomplimentary. Your job at this point is to listen. It is all right to ask questions if you don't understand what is said; or to request examples. But your goal is to listen with understanding. What you need here is additional information. You will not get it if you do all the talking or become defensive.

5. Explore career choice alternatives

In this step, you will present and discuss your career goal choices. It is to your benefit to have several career goal alternatives already identified and ready for discussion. (Do not present your action plans until the next step, since some of your goal statements may not prove feasible when examined.)

If a promotion is included in your goals, you may need to stress the need for open, honest answers. Some bosses find it difficult to be honest when there is a lack of promotional opportunity because they fear it will lower morale or upset employees.

Again, here you need to listen without interruption. Take notes if needed; and ask for clarification if you don't understand a response.

6. Create an action plan

When you arrive at an agreement on your career goal or goals, the next step is to discuss your tentative action plans as spelled out in your Career Goal Planning Work Sheet. You cannot do this, of course, if you and your boss have been unable to reach a consensus on your goals. In most cases, however, you will find that there is some match between what you want to do and what your supervisor or manager can support. If so, you will now show him or her your tentative action plan, and request help in evaluating it.

Ask your supervisor or manager for ideas on additional steps needed in your plan, and advice on any potential problems he or she sees. The goal of this discussion should be a solid action plan that has his or her support and a good chance of working.

7. Conclude the interview

To conclude the interview, tell your supervisor or manager that you are committed to making your plan work, and that you will appreciate his or her ongoing assistance. Finally, thank him or her for the time and thought given to this meeting.

8. Follow up

We sometimes begin with the best of intentions, and then experience problems because we don't follow through on our plans. You will increase the probability of achieving the goal you have agreed upon if you set a follow-up date with your supervisor or manager. The purpose of this future meeting is to discuss your progress toward completing your plan, and to deal with any new problems that may have occurred.

CONCLUSION

The career counseling interview is only the beginning of an ongoing way of managing your life in order to reach your goals. Don't put your plans in your desk drawer and forget them. Look at them at least 52 times a year. Career development is your responsibility, not anyone else's. It is up to you to make your plans work!

JOB HISTORY (page 1)

1. JOB	2. MAJOR TASKS	3. SATISFACTION LEVEL 5 = High 1 = Low	4. WHY DID YOU LIKE OR DISLIKE THIS SPECIFIC TASK? (For only the highest and lowest satisfaction levels — 5 and 1.)

JOB HISTORY (page 2)

1. JOB	2. MAJOR TASKS	3. SATISFACTION LEVEL 5 = High 1 = Low	4. WHY DID YOU LIKE OR DISLIKE THIS SPECIFIC TASK? (For only the highest and lowest satisfaction levels — 5 and 1.)

5. WHAT GENERALIZATIONS (THEMES) CAN YOU MAKE ABOUT YOURSELF FROM YOUR JOB HISTORY ANALYSIS? THAT IS, WHAT ARE THE KEY THINGS YOU WANT IN A JOB; AND WHAT THINGS DO YOU WISH TO AVOID?

LIFE HISTORY (page 1)

1. POSITIVE EVENTS (minimum of 5)	2. LIST YOUR SKILLS/ABILITIES (THAT YOU ENJOY) THAT RESULTED IN THIS EVENT.	3. WHY WAS THIS EVENT IMPORTANT TO YOU (Be honest and specific.)

LIFE HISTORY (page 2)

1. POSITIVE EVENTS
(minimum of 5)

2. LIST YOUR SKILLS/ABILITIES (THAT YOU ENJOY) THAT RESULTED IN THIS EVENT.

3. WHY WAS THIS EVENT IMPORTANT TO YOU
(Be honest and specific.)

4. FROM #2 ABOVE, LIST YOUR MOST IMPORTANT SKILLS AND ABILITIES.

5. FROM #3 ABOVE, ANALYZE THE REASONS WHY THESE EVENTS WERE PERSONALLY IMPORTANT TO YOU, AND SEE IF YOU CAN IDENTIFY YOUR UNDERLYING VALUES.

CAREER GOAL PLANNING WORK SHEET

1. Write your goal statement: _____
   _____

2. List the steps of your plan to achieve this goal:

   1. _____
   2. _____
   3. _____
   4. _____
   5. _____
   6. _____
   7. _____
   8. _____
   9. _____
   10. _____

3. Identify the step(s) with the highest risk of encountering problems (critical steps), and mark with an asterisk.

4. List the potential problems you see with the critical steps (what can go wrong?):

   Potential problems with critical step # __.

   Potential problems with critical step # __.

	P	S		P	S
_____	_	_	_____	_	_
_____	_	_	_____	_	_
_____	_	_	_____	_	_
_____	_	_	_____	_	_
_____	_	_	_____	_	_

5. Rate each potential problem as to its probability (P) and seriousness (S), using H= High, M= Medium, L= Low.

6. **Analyze each high priority (H-H, H-M, M-H) potential problem as to:**

Likely causes	Preventive action for each cause	Contingency action for each cause

7. **Repeat Steps 4–6 with any other high risk critical step (refer to Step 2).**

8. **Incorporate key preventive and contingency actions into your initial plan (Step 2) as additional needed steps.**

CHAPTER 12
MEETING CHANGE
CREATIVELY

MEETING CHANGE CREATIVELY

Change causes problems. In fact, the field of problem solving states that all problems are the product of change. Change causes **you** problems! So not only do you have to deal with outer problems resulting from change, you must also deal with the rash of emotions—fear, anxiety, and worry—that result from the changes you made to alter your life.

The emotions usually come from apprehension about the unknown. You're not sure what's coming. Or whether you can handle it. And you may fear that you are going to be less comfortable when it comes.

Human beings have different tolerances for change. While some feel overwhelmed by even the thought of making a change, others seem to thrive on change. Whatever your tolerance, this chapter is for those who must cope with change. It will show you how to increase your tolerance to change, and how to manage it to your benefit.

Many changes are positive ones. But sometimes changes don't seem to benefit you directly. In fact, you may even conclude that a change leaves you with fewer benefits, and that the change is something you are going to have to suffer through.

Your ability to *manage* change is linked to your feeling of being in control. It is also linked to the personal benefits you experience in making a change. Your challenge is to discover the ways in which a change will benefit you. Or, if there are no apparent benefits, to find strategies to control the effects of the change.

USING FORCE FIELD ANALYSIS TO MANAGE CHANGE

I used to write books longhand. And then came computers. Talk about major change! So I bought the simplest word processing program I could find, and sat down to use it. The instructions were obviously written by a computer expert, who used words I had never heard of to explain things I couldn't picture. I became so frustrated that I almost gave up. The fact that the word processing program had a built-in word speller to help me overcome my spelling problem was the only reason I stuck with it—and finally learned how to use it.

Let's use my example of the word processor computer program to illustrate the use of what is called "Force Field Analysis" (see Chapter 7) as a tool to help me analyze change—both in order to 1) gain personal control over the changes; and 2) to bring possible benefits of change (sometimes unperceived at first) into the present.

The first step is to list all the reasons—or "forces"—that support the change on one side of a vertical line, and all the opposing forces (reasons against changing) on the other side. Then use opposing arrows to represent the competing forces, with longer arrows indicating stronger forces.

FORCE FIELD ANALYSIS
Changing from Longhand to Word Processor

Forces (Reasons) for Changing	Forces (Reasons) Against Changing
Much faster	Anxiety over not knowing how to use it
Many fewer spelling errors	Initial learning time required
Don't want to appear "behind the times" to my staff	Cost of program
Easier to make changes in a document	Fear of appearing slow to learn
Electronic storage takes less space	Lost data when power is out

Now that I've learned how to use a word processor, I'll never go back to writing in longhand. But notice that I had an overwhelming reason (my need for a spell-checker) to continue in my efforts to master this new process.

Force field analysis helped me decide to make the change by graphically showing me all the factors that influenced my feelings about the change. I could see at a glance all of the positive reasons for accepting the change, as well as the ones against it. Next, I could begin to minimize the opposing forces with specific actions. For example, I could reduce the learning time required by getting somebody who knew how to use this program to show me how. His help also reduced my anxiety over not knowing how to use this new program— as well as my fear of looking like a slow learner.

A "force field" chart will help you to deal openly with your feelings about a change. It can also increase your acceptance of the need to change. This technique is especially helpful if you must cope with changes that appear to have little value. Accept the possibility that people had what they believe are good reasons for change (no matter how idiotic they might seem to you). Your job then is to uncover the reasons for change, as well as the possible benefits.

To tackle a specific change in your life, start by sketching a force field chart like the one to the left. Then write in as many benefits and disadvantages as you can think of. If the benefits side looks sparse to you, there may be some additional reasons why the change was introduced. Get more information. Go ask your boss. Inquire from peers whose opinions you respect. Talk to others outside your organization (if the change is not confidential) to get their views.

And remember your goal here: to discover, if possible, additional *positive* reasons for the change—not to affirm your own discomfort with it. Find out reasons for change so that you can support the change, if possible, from a knowledgeable position.

If you can support, or at least accept, the need for a change through knowledge, your next step is to look for ways to control the opposing forces coming from the change. That will help you to cope with the changes—constructively, creatively, and even, as is often done, to your advantage.

CAUSES OF CHANGE

Being motivated to accept change is only the first step. Once we say, "OK, I see the need for this change," the next thing we must do is figure out how and what we must change. And how we implement our personal changes depends on the kinds of larger change we are facing.

EXTERNAL CHANGE

External changes originate outside of your organization. These are the ones that can cause you the most mental distress, because they often cause a feeling of loss of control. For example, if the economy turns downward, and your organization starts to lay off its workers, it can be difficult to feel you are in control of your future.

There are five major causes of external change:

1. New technology.

2. Governmental regulations.

3. Variable economy.

4. Job mobility.

5. Personal relationships.

Let's look at each of these causes of external change.

New technology can cause havoc within any organization. Although it is rare that new technology results in industry-wide layoffs, it can cause great disruption in a particular organization. Even if you don't lose your job, you may still feel anxiety over the possibility of being retrained, or moving to another job.

However, new technology can result in a job that is even more secure. Suppose your organization, for example, decides to reorganize its reporting procedures, and therefore installs a new system of computers to speed the flow of information. As a result, you are given hundreds of hours of training to teach you how to use the new equipment. This additional training and your new skill make you even more valuable to your organization than before.

Governmental regulations can also have a high impact on organizations. Affirmative action, tax regulations, automotive emission and gas consumption regulations, waste water disposal guidelines, and safety regulations are all examples of laws and regulations that have caused major changes and resulting problems within organizations.

But even changes in governmental regulations can result in opportunities. As an example, look at what has happened to the automobile industry. Continued change in the government's regulations with regard to automotive gasoline has resulted in the development of high-efficiency engines that are among the best in the world. The net effect of this has been to help save jobs by making the U.S. more competitive in world markets.

Variable economy. Inflation, stagnation, depression, Third World debt, balance of payments, national debt, and competition from a world market are all economic realities of our time. Since you have little chance of preventing any of these problems, the way to reduce your anxiety over their occurrence is to take action ahead of time to protect yourself when they occur.

Note that I said "when," not "if," they occur. Large-scale economic changes have happened, are happening, and will continue to happen. Since you know that you will experience some, or even all, of the global economic problems mentioned above, and that they will have a profound effect on your organization, then it is to your benefit to do those things now that will help you cope with a problem when it occurs. For example, increase your savings rate. Cut back on high-interest charge accounts. Reduce your expenses. Get a part-time job and save the extra money.

Make yourself even more valuable to your organization by increasing the quality and quantity of your output. Add to your knowledge and skills so you can do other, more secure, jobs. The employees who survive swings in the economy are those who are the least dispensable to their organizations. You'll find it is much easier to make such changes in your personal situation now than after trouble comes.

Job mobility has both positive and negative consequences. It is nice to be able to move from an organization that is in trouble to one that is thriving. But such a move can also be traumatic. New bosses and associates, new procedures and policies, or simply the new location can all add up to stress.

Change is best managed by preparation. For instance, if you decide to move to a new organization, the following are some of the important things you can do. If you belong to a professional society, become more active. Arrange, if possible, to talk with people who work (or used to work) in the new organization. You can also contact the personnel department of the new organization and ask for a brochure or pamphlet on the history of the organization. If such information is not available in writing, ask for the name and telephone number of an older employee and call him or her direct. Such a contact is invaluable in that you can learn about the organization and the unwritten do's and don'ts.

You may even find it possible to ask your prospective boss to give you information on the people you will be working with—e.g., what they do in their jobs, how they might interact with you, and even their hobbies and outside interests. This will help you establish links of interest so that when you arrive it will be easier to make friends. In other words, the more you know about your future job, the organization, and the people you will be working with, the more comfortable and effective your transition will be.

Personal relationships. The final major external factor causing change—one which we must all cope with—is personal relationships. Marital problems, separation, divorce, alcohol or drug-dependent family members, children leaving home, death—all are examples of external situations that can cause untold stress and change in our lives. The best advice in dealing with such changes is to get professional help; and, if possible, group support. It is far better to seek help than to try to "tough it out" by yourself. There are many things you can personally do to cope positively with severe stress in personal relationships, but experience shows that trained resource people outside the situation are often required for success.

INTERNAL CHANGE

External forces cause internal organizational changes—sometimes sweeping ones. But other changes within an organization are caused by internal initiatives. These actions fall into three categories: personnel changes, job changes, and organizational changes. Let's look at each of these in turn.

Personnel changes can have a strong impact on our ability to cope. Suppose you get a new boss; or a good friend leaves the organization; or a new employee is hired and assigned to work with you. All of these changes can be difficult to manage.

When bosses change, people understandably get apprehensive. What will the new boss be like? What will be his or her expectations of you? Even if your old boss was headed for first prize as a Worst Boss of the Year, you still may feel concern about what the new boss will be like. And, of course, it is even worse if you had an extremely good relationship with your old supervisor or manager.

There are always things you can do to cope constructively with personnel changes. For example, new bosses have histories—they come from somewhere. The odds are that your new boss was promoted from within your organization. If so, it is fairly easy to talk to his or her previous employees and obtain information to fill in some of the unknown picture. You can even take the initiative and set up a meeting with your new supervisor or manager. In this meeting, tell him or her about your job tasks, and decide how these tasks fit into the overall goal of the department or section. Then ask for feedback.

Losing a friendly co-worker can also be distressing. In general, close relationships that develop on the job do not normally continue when one of the individuals leaves. You have at least two options in managing the change that occurs when a co-worker who is also a friend leaves your area or organization. First, the two of you can deliberately plan outside activities, or develop common interests that have nothing to do with work. This will allow you to maintain a continuing relationship, even though you no longer work together.

Or, if you find you must give up the relationship, it is important to permit yourself to grieve over the loss. For example, I once had a wonderful boss, an ex-football player who was a mountain of a man with a heart of gold. And I liked him a great deal. But because our boss-subordinate roles had not allowed for a friendship off the job, we could not maintain our relationship when I resigned my position and took another job. I permitted myself to experience fully the sadness and deep sense of loss that this change brought about. And this open acknowledgment of my feelings helped—though I miss him still.

Another type of change occurs when an employee you don't know is assigned to work with you. If this employee is a new hire, then your role may be to help him or her learn the job. Or possibly this is an employee who was transferred into your section against his or her wishes. Probably he or she is anxious about the new job. Therefore, your role is to help him or her overcome the anxiety in order to manage the change as smoothly as possible.

Since you know this person is probably nervous and anxious about the new job, do not say, "This job is simple. You'll catch on in no time." Rather than relieving tension, this can make it worse—since by stating that the job is "easy" you are in effect saying that the person is not very smart if he or she experiences difficulty. Better to say something like, "I know that most new jobs appear difficult. But I am confident that you can manage it."

You can also help new employees overcome some of their anxiety by finding out what their outside interests are. Then introduce them to others in your section or department, indicating "links" of common interest.

Job changes can also have major effects on us. Such changes can range from the addition of a new job task to a new job due to promotion or transfer. The key word here is "new." The more a new job is unlike your old one, the greater can be your anxiety. So when you are assigned a completely new job, you can expect to feel anxious about it.

A key strategy here is to make all the tasks of the new job clearly visible. That is, ask the person who is responsible for your training to write out your job tasks on a sheet of paper. Then review each task with the trainer, and write out an on-the-job training plan. This will take some of the mystery out of the unfamiliar assignment, and place you more in control. It will help you to see that what, at first, may appear to be an overwhelming job is really a series of particular tasks which you are able to carry out.

Organizational changes often cause us deep concern about our future. Some of the types of changes that affect our organizations, like external technological or economic ones, have already been considered. But there are also internally caused changes that organizations make. They want to be more competitive, introduce a new product or service, increase their profit, reduce operating expenses, pay bigger dividends to their stockholders, or even simply look good in the eyes of a new administration. But whatever the organizational change, you are almost certain to be affected by it in some way.

There are several types of organizational change. New equipment, new processes, and new policies and procedures can all bring about organizational changes—which may profoundly affect your job. The best way to meet such change is by being assertive about your right to know what is going on. Speak with your boss, the personnel department, or even your department's director. Most of our concern about organizational changes is due to our not being kept informed. The more we can find out the specifics of a change from informed people, the better we will feel and function. Here, of course, you must be careful about the "rumor mill." Organizational changes tend to produce strange rumors. So make every effort to obtain your information from those people who, in fact, know the facts.

GUIDELINES FOR MANAGING CHANGE

Several guidelines stand out clearly when we ask how to manage change well.

- First, changes almost always have significant personal benefits. Your job is to identify these benefits and to use them to create within yourself a genuine, productive acceptance of a change.

- Secondly, don't become paralyzed by change. Figure out what aspects of the situation you can control and take positive action on those parts. Even the effects of a change that appear most negative can sometimes be turned to your advantage, when you take charge creatively in the areas you still control.

- Finally, seek the assistance of others. The simple act of talking to someone who is a good listener is sometimes all that is needed to reduce your anxiety to a manageable level and to free your energy.

And above all, even if an organizational change seems overwhelming or impossible for you to accept, don't quit your job in a huff! Give yourself time to manage the change.

If you still choose to leave your organization, then take the time to look for another job before you quit. Most people find that it is much easier to obtain another job while they are already holding one. The plain fact is that, as a rule, you are more highly valued by prospective employers if you are employed, and less valued if you are not.

Again, remember the two major objectives in managing change: 1) look for the benefits, and 2) take control. On the following page is a work sheet to use for managing the changes that are affecting you.

MANAGING CHANGE WORK SHEET

1. Write a brief description below of the change that concerns you.

   _____

   _____

   _____

2. Using the force field chart below, list the reasons, or forces, that support the change on the left side, and the opposing forces on the right. Place an arrow over each force, with its length indicating the strength of the force (reason).

Forces for Changing	Forces Against Changing

3. What information do you need to further complete the chart above?

   _____

   _____

   _____

4. Who has the needed information?_____

   _____

5. What are the major benefits of this change for *you*?

_____

_____

_____

_____

6. What specific things can you do about the opposing forces (negative results) that will minimize, or even reverse, their effects, putting you in better control?

_____

_____

_____

_____

_____

7. What additional actions will you need to take to make this change work beneficially for you?

_____

_____

_____

_____

_____

_____

CHAPTER 13
BEING MANAGED

I have thought a lot about what to title this final chapter. "Developing a Good Relationship with Your Manager or Supervisor," "You and Your Manager," "Managing Your Boss," and even "Becoming Indispensable" were my first thoughts. I settled on "Being Managed." In this chapter I'll give you common sense ideas that you can use to enhance your relationship with your boss. And I have chosen to do this by looking at what I think bosses really want from their employees. So let's pretend that I am your new supervisor.

Now that we are working together, I'd like to tell you privately about my expectations. I have reserved this conference room, hung a "Meeting in Progress" sign on the door, and asked my secretary to see that we are not interrupted. Would you like a cup of coffee? OK. Let's get started.

First, and most important, I want you to know what my expectations are concerning the way I would like us to communicate with one another. Next, I will briefly review my expectations about work habits in this department. And finally, I would like to talk about your job. Oh, not your particular assignment—but what I want from all my employees as they work in this department. So let's start with communications—and talk about the way you communicate with me.

COMMUNICATION

First, keep me informed. Tell me not only the good news, but the bad news as well. The worst news is bad news that was suppressed until the situation became a disaster. If you tell me the bad news as soon as possible, we'll have more time to handle the problem. This will also prevent my boss from hearing about it before I do. It's very disturbing to have my boss walk up and ask, "What's this I hear about a problem in your section?" when I don't have any idea what he is talking about.

The next thing I need is to know that what you say to me is the truth. I know this may sound odd; but I couldn't be more sincere. Let's look at an example. Suppose that last night my wife and I celebrated our anniversary, and didn't get to bed until late. Because of my lack of sleep, I overslept the this morning. An hour late for work, I pulled into the parking lot, ran inside the building, slowed down as I saw my boss in the hallway—and said, "Sorry I'm late, boss, but I had car trouble."

Now if I had told this lie, it would have demonstrated how unimportant my own character was to me. And it would have shown how little I cared about my boss. As I see it, people who lie about little things will also lie about important things. In order for me to do my job, my employees must have the courage to be straight with me. I'll help you in any way I can. I'll go to bat for you with management. I will always try to be a person you can count on. But please don't lie to me! I can't trust people who lie, and I don't want to work with people I can't trust.

If I ask you to do something and you don't understand what I said, please ask me to explain what I meant. I'd much rather try to explain something more clearly than have you get in trouble because I didn't do a very good job of communicating. If you don't understand what I say, the chances are I didn't communicate as well as I should. So it's not a reflection on you if I have to restate my instructions. It is only a reflection on you if you nod wisely while thinking, "What in the world is he asking me to do?"

I also expect you to let me know what you need to do your job better. I may not always be able to do what you want. But I will listen with respect. If I can't do what you ask, I'll tell you why. Also, let me know what you like about your job and what you want to keep the same. Sometimes it can seem like all I hear are the gripes. It's really helpful if you tell me about the positive things as well.

I would also like you to have the courage to let me know how I can be a better manager for you. Like most people, I'm sensitive to criticism. So simply be tactful when you give me feedback. By that, I mean if I do something that makes you angry, wait and cool off before letting me know about it. But tell me when you think I'm wrong, or about to do something wrong. I value your opinion. And be specific. Try to avoid generalities like, "You never tell me when I do something well!" When someone makes a sweeping statement like that, I naturally become defensive. It may be true that I don't give enough positive feedback. But by using the word "never," the statement is very likely untrue.

A far better statement would be to say, "I felt good about the work I did on the Adams report. But when I gave it to you yesterday, I was disappointed that I didn't receive some positive comment on what I did." With this comment, you are not blaming or judging me. Instead, you are objectively describing a specific incident that occurred, expressing your feelings about it, and stating what you want. You see, most bosses don't walk around asking, "How can I be nasty to my people today?" More often than not, we simply don't realize it when we say something inappropriate. So if you can let me know tactfully, I'll really try to do better the next time.

Also, have the courage to let me know what you like about the way I manage. I know there are all kinds of labels for people who butter up the boss. But I'm not talking about flattery for the purpose of making points with the boss. I am talking about the courage to be able to say sincerely, "I like what you did, because..." This lets me know what you appreciate about what I'm doing—and increases the chances that I will continue doing it.

Instead of spreading a rumor, I trust that you will let me know what you have heard. This gives me the opportunity to check it out and let you know what is fact and what is fiction. Rumors are really deadly; they can cause terrible morale problems. And because rumors are usually distorted versions of truth, they have a special power to upset people.

To sum up these thoughts on communication, I want you to do just that with me—communicate! Communicate good news and bad news. Have the courage to let me know how I can be a better manager for you. If you don't understand a job assignment, ask me. If you need something to do your job better, ask me. In many ways you are much closer to the work in our area than I am. As a result I must depend on you for accurate, timely communication.

WORK HABITS

What can I say about work habits? Come to work on time. Take appropriate breaks. Work when you are supposed to work. Do your job to the best of your ability. If you don't, then I'll have to talk with you about improving your work habits. And do you know something? I hate to have to discipline employees! I worry about having to do it; I feel distress about what I'll have to say and how I'll say it; and I worry about how the employee will receive it. In short, having to counsel employees about poor work habits wastes both employee and boss time.

I once had an employee who had graduated at the top of his university class. He was a super-nice guy, and could do almost anything. But he had a problem. He was supposed to be on the job at 9:00, but often didn't show up until 10:00 or 10:30. He would leave work to go get a pizza, and would straggle back an hour and a half later. At 4:00 I'd go to look for him and find he had left early.

About every two weeks I would have to sit down with him and talk about his work habits. He would assure me that he would improve. But several weeks later he would fall back into his old habits. That man ruined more of my days than I care to remember. Finally I was forced to admit failure and terminate his services.

So get in the habit of developing good work habits—even with jobs that don't excite you. And it's not that hard to do. Just take things one day at a time. Decide that you don't want the anxiety caused by not getting to work on time. Eliminate excessive break time and too-long lunches. In other words, resolve to give an honest day's work. After all, the organization pays you, and it has a right to expect your best for its money. Keep your work area clean and well organized. And if safety is important in your job, make job safety your life goal. In other words, commit to good work habits—to make both of our days positive and productive.

YOUR JOB

The last thing I want to express is my expectations about your job performance. As I said when we started, I'm not talking about the details of how you do your job. What I want to talk about is the way you and I interact around your job.

First, always try to bring me suggestions for solving a problem, not just the problem. Please don't come and ask me what to do about a problem. Spend a few minutes thinking it through, analyzing what might be the causes, and considering some solutions. Then when you come to see me, you can say, "Boss, we have a serious problem with X. But I think if we do Y or Z, we can resolve it." Look at problems as opportunities to do things differently and better.

Next, do express your ideas. There is no way that I can have all the answers about your job. So I am counting on you to think of new and better ways of doing what we have always done. There might be a reason why a certain idea won't work; and if so, I'll explain the reason. But since you're closer to your job than I can possibly be, most new ideas need to come from you.

Because you will know your work better than anyone else, I encourage you to plan. Take some time to figure out what you want to accomplish in your job. Then write out several key goals and objectives, and make detailed plans for each one. When you've done so, set up a meeting with me to review your plans. By doing this, you take charge of your job. And I can see better how to help you get what you need.

One last thing before we call it a day. **If you run out of something to do, I'll appreciate it if you come and ask me if there is additional work available.** It's very distressing to see an employee sleeping at his or her desk, or standing around with nothing to do and taking up other people's time with chitchat. My personal feeling—and I know it is shared by most managers and supervisors—is that to be paid for what we are *not* doing is simply stealing money from our organization!

I hope you don't feel that I've gotten on a soapbox! My goal in everything I've shared here is to help you be genuinely successful in your job as we work together. By following these few important guidelines, you'll find that you will experience the pride and fulfillment of being a self-directed, respected co-worker whom others— including me—will increasingly depend on. Good luck! And whenever you have questions, please let me know.

CONCLUSION

After reading this chapter, you might think, "Yeah, but you don't know my boss!" And you are partly right—I don't know your boss. But I can assure you that if you do your best with even the worst boss, you will likely see dramatic results. You owe it to your self-pride to give your job your best. And your best will almost certainly produce benefits—for your boss, your organization, and for you!

CHAPTER 14
CONCLUSION

Why is it that some people feel their coffee break is the best part of their day? Who started the myth that the only time you can feel good about what you do is when you're on a break? Who said that work has to be dull and deadening to your spirit? Look at some synonyms for work: toil, labor, drudgery, grind!

Did our Old World heritage start this depressing litany? Maybe. There was a time when grimfaced men, women and children trudged off to dark, dirty factories for 60- or 70-hour work weeks. Work in those days **was** "toil, labor, drudgery, and grind."

But not today! Not in this country, nor in most other modern countries. Times have changed. And it is time for the myth of "work as drudgery" to change. Your work can be fun, not drudgery. It can provide pleasure and enjoyment, and it can give deep personal satisfaction. But only if this is what you want.

This book is for those who want to take pride in what they do and pleasure in doing their best. I have tried to provide you with practical ideas to use in making yourself even more effective on the job. And as you read these ideas, you might have discovered common themes. These themes are my personal values, which form a foundation for the ideas that are presented.

So to summarize this book, I'd like to state my values. I believe the following things to be true:

1. Work can be fun! If I must work eight hours a day, and only get two ten-minute coffee breaks, then *work* should be the best part of my day—and **can** be!.

2. I must take responsibility for myself. I can't blame my friends, my boss, the organization, my country, the world, or aliens for my problems. I have the power to change myself to cope more effectively with my environment.

3. What I do or don't do on the job does make a difference.

4. Large results in my performance are obtained by many small changes.

5. Problems are really opportunities to do things differently and better.

6. What I think of others is often dependent on what I think of myself.

7. My job in life is to be true to myself, and true to others.

8. What I think I do and what I really do are often different. Therefore, I need specific feedback from others to determine the reality of my performance.

9. I can learn more by listening than by talking.

10. I can learn more by asking than by telling.

11. My co-workers deserve my respect, courtesy, and concern.

12. If I take my organization's money for the work I do, then I owe it my best.

Maybe my values appear to be a bit old-fashioned. That's OK. I've seen old-fashioned values like these make people, organizations, and countries genuinely successful.

Best wishes to you as you strive to be the best you can be!

Dick Leatherman

Dick Leatherman is President and CEO of International Training Consultants, a major vendor of training packages, videos, and needs assessment instrumentation.

Dick has designed and written hundreds of effective training programs, and he continues to be much sought-after as a seminar leader and lecturer. He now dedicates much of his time to research and development projects, designing new training materials for ITC's expanding market.

Dick is widely recognized for his pioneering work in the areas of trainer training and needs assessment instrumentation. His published instrument, the Leatherman Leadership Questionnaire (or LLQ), is considered state-of-the art.

Prior to founding ITC, Dick served as Manager of Education and Training for 3M Corporation. Dick attended the University of Minnesota and holds an M.A. and Ph.D. from Virginia Commonwealth University.